PENGUIN BOOKS
IGNITED MINDS

A.P.J. Abdul Kalam (1931–2015) was one of India's most distinguished scientists. He was responsible for the development of India's first satellite launch vehicle, the SLV-3, and the development and operationalization of strategic missiles. As chairman of the Technology Information, Forecasting and Assessment Council, he pioneered India Vision 2020, a road map for transforming India into an economically developed nation by 2020, focusing on PURA (Provision of Urban Amenities in Rural Areas) as a development system for countrywide implementation.

Kalam held various positions in the Indian Space Research Organisation and the Defence Research and Development Organisation and became principal scientific adviser to the Government of India, holding the rank of a cabinet minister.

The President of India between 2002 and 2007, Kalam was awarded honorary doctorates from thirty-eight universities and the country's three highest civilian honours—Padma Bhushan (1981), Padma Vibhushan (1990) and Bharat Ratna (1997).

Kalam authored fifteen books on a variety of topics that have been translated into many languages across the world. His most significant works are *Wings of Fire*, *India 2020: A Vision for the New Millennium*, *Target 3 Billion* and *Beyond 2020: A Vision for Tomorrow's India*.

PRAISE FOR THE BOOK

'The strength of *Ignited Minds* . . . lies in the scientist's ability to present some of the most tangled issues that confront the nation in easily digestible packages of information.'
—Raj Chengappa in *India Today*

'Kalam is a dreamer of great dreams . . . *Ignited Minds* will fire the minds of the young to whom it is primarily addressed.'
—Khushwant Singh in *Outlook*

'It is not possible in [a] short review to convey the vast erudition of a man who covers so much of India's past, present and future in such simple, communicable terms. Or his many revolutionary as well as practical ideas for the country which he so obviously loves, of which he is so proud and which he feels can be the country of his dreams by 2020.'
—Amita Malik in *Hindu*

'*Ignited Minds* is a book to be read by the leaders and led, by young as well as old and by all who love their country . . . Kalam [dares] to say what has long needed to be said but which has gone unsaid . . .'
—M.V. Kamath in *Sentinel*

'*Ignited Minds* is a lucid and elegant expression of [Kalam's] dreams about India's future . . . This is a feel-good book. It is a true patriot's self-help guide to a better nation.'
—Wilson John in *Pioneer*

A.P.J. ABDUL KALAM

IGNITED MINDS

UNLEASHING THE POWER WITHIN INDIA

PENGUIN BOOKS

An imprint of Penguin Random House

PENGUIN BOOKS

USA | Canada | UK | Ireland | Australia
New Zealand | India | South Africa | China

Penguin Books is part of the Penguin Random House group of companies
whose addresses can be found at global.penguinrandomhouse.com

Published by Penguin Random House India Pvt. Ltd
7th Floor, Infinity Tower C, DLF Cyber City,
Gurgaon 122 002, Haryana, India

 Penguin
Random House
India

First published in Viking by Penguin Books India 2002
Published in Penguin Books 2003
This edition published 2014

Copyright © A.P.J. Abdul Kalam 2002

27

ISBN 9780143424123

Typeset in Nebraska by SÜRYA, New Delhi
Printed at Thomson Press India Ltd, New Delhi

www.penguin.co.in

I dedicate this book to a child who is studying in class 12. Her name is Snehal Thakkar. On 11 April 2002 when I reached Anand by road in the evening, it was under curfew following communal disturbances. The next day, at the Anandalaya High School, while talking to the students, a question came up: 'Who is our enemy?'

There were many answers, but the one we all agreed was correct came from her. 'Our enemy is poverty.'

It is the root cause of our problems and should be the object of our fight, not our own.

CONTENTS

PREFACE

Nations consist of people. And with their effort a nation can accomplish all it could ever want. Motivating India's people, and its youth especially, is the central theme of *Ignited Minds,* which continues the trajectory of thoughts taken up in my earlier two books, *Wings of Fire* and *India 2020: A Vision for the New Millennium,* written with my friends Arun Tiwari and Y.S. Rajan. I have chosen to write about this subject of igniting young minds so that India turns into a developed nation by the year 2020 because all through my career in the field of technology and its management, I relied on the power and potential of youth. My strength has been my young teams who never let me down. And what satisfaction there was in working with them on some of the most complex projects in some of the most challenging situations! Given the freedom to achieve and guided properly, I am convinced the young of India can accomplish far more.

As I began writing, I wondered if I was not overreaching myself. I thought: Who am I to write about this capacity of India to realize its destiny as a developed nation? What do I really know about how this can be accomplished beyond what I have learned in my projects and missions evolved around science and technology? Isn't this an area that political leaders, economists, thinkers and other competent people would address better? How am I qualified to tell others about an ability that has been generally ignored?

At first as I was putting down my experiences with youth, I had no idea of what I would have to say. However, I put aside my doubts and began to examine what I hear from the people I meet during my visits to different places, particularly children, saints and seers, teachers, scientists, industry leaders and even political leaders. I am sure on my part that India has the ability to transform itself into a developed nation. Through my projects in space, defence and nuclear sectors, I know that our people have the ability to achieve the best in the world. They have a fantastic mix of belief and knowledge that sets them apart from any other nation on earth. I also know that their potential has gone untapped because we have become used to being subjugated and docile. What better project can I undertake than to tell my people that what they dream of can become possible, that they can have anything that comprises a good life: health, education, the freedom to pursue their goals, and above all, peace.

My quest for answers as to how this could be done took me to schools, the countryside, ashrams and many other places which were not part of my itinerary earlier. It was a new kind of experience, a very stimulating one at that. The paddy fields in Bihar left to an ad-hoc cycle of agriculture, the untapped mineral wealth of the newly formed state of Jharkhand and the unattended biodiversity of Tripura are throwing a great challenge to the knowledge era that is dawning.

In Assam the sight of the mighty Brahmaputra almost mesmerized me. Its vast expanse of water filled me with a strange sense of helplessness too—the river's untapped flow was taking a gigantic mass of water into the sea. It made me think, that as a nation too we were failing to utilize our tremendous energies.

Where are we making a mistake? What is it that needs to be corrected? We have a roadmap in our five-year plans that covers some of the things we need to achieve. We have most of the necessary resources. There seems to be an attitude problem, as if we cannot shake ourselves out of a mindset of limited achievement. This book is all about breaking away from the forces that would prefer us to remain a nation of a billion people selling cheap labour and raw materials and providing a large market for goods and services of other nations.

I am writing this book to make my young readers hear a voice that says, 'Start moving.' Leadership must lead us to prosperity. Young Indians with constructive ideas should not have to see them wither in the long wait for approval. They have to rise above norms which are meant to keep them timid in the name of safety and to discourage entrepreneurship in the name of trade regimes, organizational order and group behaviour. As it is said, Thinking is the capital, Enterprise is the way, Hard Work is the solution.

Every nation has struggled to achieve its goals. Generations have given their best to make life better for their offspring. There is nothing mysterious or hidden about this, no alternative to effort. And yet we fail to follow the winning track. More than the problems outside—globalization, recession, inflation, insurgency, instability and so on—I am concerned about the inertia that has gripped the national psyche, the mindset of defeat. I believe that when we believe in our goals, that what we dream of can become reality, results will begin to follow. *Ignited Minds* is about developing that conviction in ourselves, and discarding the things that hold us back.

This was, in fact, a central thought that I kept in mind as I wrote. Share my dream of a developed India and see it made real in your own and others' lives. In my own way, I have tried to follow my beliefs, to do what I loved doing. I have tried, however, to guide but not to impose my views on others.

You will find in this book plain speaking: Surge ahead as a developed nation or perish in perpetual poverty, subservient to a few countries that control the world politically and economically. There are no other alternatives.

In the nine chapters of this book, I take up various themes. I begin with a rumination on peace, without which there can be no progress, and on the shift in the direction of my own life that occurred after surviving a helicopter crash. There is a chapter based on my interaction with children all over India. Other chapters contain the insights I gained in my meetings with saints and seers, scientists, outstanding thinkers and others. There are accounts of some promising experiments in agriculture and in the medical field. Elsewhere I deal with concepts that carry the seed of solutions. The contents essentially come from the people of this nation, from what they have taught me.

I have written this book as an expression of my faith in the potential of India and my countrymen. We have all the resources we need, whether it be people, talent, natural bounty or other assets. India is truly blessed with a real, though latent, abundance. Scarcity of resources is not the cause of our problems. Our problems originate in our approach towards them. We are spreading our resources too wide and too thin. With our resources and the money we spend we could easily accomplish three times what we do, in half the time we normally take, if we were to operate in mission mode with a vision for the nation. The vision generates the best in every field.

We must change tracks. It is imperative that our policy making become more responsive and efficient so that the stifled entrepreneurship is liberated. Key to that is better coordination among the various departments, rather than emphasis on priorities according to the preferences of individual departments. There are more reviews than views available. Every channel appears blocked by some obstacle or the other. The trapped energies and the suppressed initiative need to be freed and properly harnessed. Nor do we particularly need every time to borrow models from elsewhere. I don't think the American, Japanese or Singaporean solutions will work for us. Knocking at others' doors will be futile. Instead of importing theories and transplanting concepts we need to grow our own solutions. Instead of searching for answers outside we will have to look within for them.

I hope that when you go through these nine chapters you will be given the guidance that I got from the people of my country and feel connected to the wisdom that is so special to this soil. The reality of a developed nation will become part of your daily life. Twenty years from now I may not be around. But I am sure many of you will be there to share in the glory of success and agree that I was right in being so confident.

Many friends and associates helped me put this book together. I am grateful to them all. My special thanks to Mr Y.S. Rajan, and Dr M.S. Vijayaraghavan for shaping my thoughts with their vital inputs. Dr A. Sivathanu Pillai has worked with me for a long time and his contribution has been both timely and invaluable in giving shape to ideas and thoughts. I am fortunate to have his friendship. I am grateful to

Mr H. Sheridon who directly keyed in my dictations into his laptop computer with outstanding skill. My co-author in *Wings of Fire*, Mr Arun K. Tiwari, did his usual craftsmanship with words on the manuscript and I appreciate every bit of that. It was a great pleasure to work with Mr Krishan Chopra of Penguin Books. From the emanation of my thoughts to the book's realization, his constant interaction was of great support.

Chennai   A.P.J. Abdul Kalam
April 2002

ACKNOWLEDGEMENTS

I have listed some of the books that were useful to me in the writing of this book. I would like to mention three books whose ideas I found specially relevant to my theme. They were *Chandra: A Biography of S. Chandrasekhar* by Kameshwar C. Wali, Penguin Books; *Empires of the Mind* by Denis Waitley, Nicholas Brealey Publishing; and *Manifest Your Destiny* by Dr Wayne W. Dyer, HarperCollins. Some of Dr Dyer's ideas on individual achievement I found useful in addressing the theme of a nation's awakening to its potential. The other books that I consulted are listed in the references.

1

THE DREAM AND THE MESSAGE

Dream, Dream, Dream
Dreams transform into thoughts
And thoughts result in action.

On 30 September 2001, I was on my way to Bokaro
from Ranchi in Jharkhand when the helicopter carrying
me crashed moments before landing. It hit the earth
with a thud after its engine failed. All of us on board
had a miraculous escape. Grateful to God but unfazed
by the incident, I went ahead with my scheduled
programme of addressing the students in Bokaro. At
night, however, a panel of doctors persuaded me to

take a tranquillizer to alleviate my perceived shock. The drug made me sleep hours ahead of my usual time—1 a.m. I also failed to rise at my usual 6 a.m. and woke up only after eight o'clock.

It was, however, a disturbed sleep, and sometime in the middle of it, I fell to thinking why the human race, the best of all of God's creations, has been so deeply divided by violence. I imagined a conversation between five people who together symbolize the finest attributes of the human mind and whom I admire deeply. Through their conversation, I sought an answer. In this experience, much more intense and vivid than a dream, though for want of a better word I shall term it that, I saw myself in a desert with miles of sand all around. There was a full moon and the desert was bathed in its light. Five men—Mahatma Gandhi, Albert Einstein, Emperor Asoka, Abraham Lincoln and Caliph Omar—stood in a circle, their clothes ruffled by the wind.

I felt myself dwarfed standing next to the majestic Emperor Asoka. Asoka led two lives, one as a ruthless conqueror and the other as a compassionate ruler. The man I stood beside was the one who had just returned from conquest. But victory had been obtained at heavy cost: the battle of Kalinga claimed the lives of at least 300,000 people and an equal number were wounded. I saw everyone looking at Asoka who fell on his knees and removed his armour and crown. His face was pale, reflecting the death surrounding him. He looked at the sky. He saw the bright cool moon shining and God's grace pouring down on mother earth. And he looked down at the horror he had created, making blood flow everywhere. In that moment of beauty and horror—the silver moonlight and the suffering and pain on the ground, when Nature itself seemed to speak out against what he had wrought, Ahimsa Dharma was born. Emperor Asoka embraced God's command to propagate love for human beings through this doctrine.

As I stood by, I wondered. Why the Kalinga war, why the assassination of Mahatma Gandhi and of Abraham Lincoln? Or many others like them? Has God Almighty faltered in His Creation? Is the destruction of mankind essential for a Second Creation?

In that blissful silence the Mahatma spoke, 'Friends, the divine message we are hearing is the message of creation. Since we all belong to planet earth, we may give a message to mankind, how people of different races, religions and languages can live peacefully and prosperously together.

'God Almighty has blessed us all with something unique that we passed on to mankind through our deeds and efforts. Is that working? Is there any divine message or doctrine? Divine beauty should enter the human soul and happiness blossom in the body and mind. Is it possible?'

Asoka said, 'Friends, there is one thing I have realized, there is no victory in causing suffering. Triumph is a peaceful kingdom.'

Caliph Omar said, 'I learned after I entered Jerusalem that all men are equal. There is no point in forcing others to follow your path. You will get only that which is ordained for you. God alone is the sovereign.'

Caliph Omar never saw his position in terms of the special privileges that it carried. To him government was a sacred trust and he did his best not to betray that trust in any way.

It was Einstein's turn. 'I would like to recall my friend Werner Heisenberg's view, "You know, in the West we have built a large, beautiful ship. It has all the comforts in it, but one thing is missing: it has no compass and does not know where to go. Men like Tagore and Gandhi and their spiritual forebears found the compass. Why can this compass not be put in the human ship so that both can realize their purpose?"'

Abraham Lincoln, the great American leader who fought against slavery and whose life paralleled that of the Mahatma in certain respects, said at this point, 'There is one thing that I would like to say: happiness comes from a family's prosperity at various levels. God's grace gives bliss to human lives. Happiness and bliss are two important components of a godly life on earth. Perhaps there is so much conflict between peoples and nations because in our pursuit of prosperity and power we have lost sight of ethical values. We must ask ourselves, what is the role of human consciousness? Does it have a part in political thinking, scientific thinking and theological thinking? Is spirituality acceptable in the business of life?'

Mahatma Gandhi recalled sage Ashtavakra who propounded, '"Oh my son! You are the very Consciousness within which arises this phenomenal universe that is not separate from what you are. How can there be a question of anything being acceptable or unacceptable?" Let the business of life be peace and prosperity, and not exploitation and conflict.

'This is our message to the planet. Everything that we do, any doctrine that we espouse, should be for the good of humankind.'

The next morning I kept sitting for some time drinking my tea and pondering about this strange dream. What if the helicopter had lost power at some more height? Just a few hours before my own mishap, a plane carrying a promising leader and a team of young and talented journalists had crashed, killing all. I had been lucky to survive and now there was the night's experience that seemed to hold a message for me. What should I do?

I looked out of the window. The sun was well up in the sky and there was a soothing breeze. I have always lived in close touch with nature and have always found it a friend, giving without reservation, like the mango tree—people throw stones at it, break off its branches, but it still offers its shade to the weary traveller, and its fruit to the hungry. Whether it was the sea at Rameswaram, Thumba and Chandipur; the desert at Pokhran; or the gigantic boulders in Hyderabad, nature has always made its presence felt wherever I have worked. It has helped to remind me of the divine force that pervades all of creation.

I kept on pondering over my dream. And yet, the history of the world shows the forces of good struggling hard to make life better for mankind while the human race also shows a terrible capacity for destruction. Thus we have Gandhi, and other great saints and teachers who lay down the precepts for a happy and virtuous life, on the one hand, and on the other the death of millions in the Second World War and the dropping of atomic bombs that destroyed entire cities. Thousands have died in the Bosnia conflict, the Israel–Palestine conflict continues to take lives, and on 11 September 2001 terrorists used a new tactic to take lives when they struck at the World Trade Center in New York. At home, in the Bhopal gas tragedy, 30,000 people died as the result of the carelessness of a multinational company, and thousands more have died in the Kashmir Valley violence. On 13 December 2001, when the leaders of India were in Parliament, an attempt was made by the terrorists to paralyse the country. Where will it all stop? Are we doomed to destroy ourselves? No, we have to find an everlasting solution.

I recall a poem I wrote a few years ago,
'The Tree of Life'.

'You, the human race are the best of my creations
You will live and live,
And give and give till you are united,
In happiness and pain!
My bliss will be born in you,
Love is a continuum,
That is the mission of humanity,
You will see every day in the Life Tree.
You learn and learn,

8

My best of creations.'

The five great human beings I saw in my dream lived at different times. In the modern world, there are few examples of human beings who embody the qualities that come from realizing the nature of the mind. Once a child asked me if I had read the Mahabharata and if so, who my favourite character in it was. The multifaceted characters in the epic represent almost every aspect of human nature, good as well as bad. I told the child that I was particularly attracted to the character of Vidura, who showed grit against the wrongdoings of authority and had the courage to differ when everyone else chose to surrender before the tyranny of adharma.

Today, it is hard for us to find one true Vidura among our leaders. It is hard for us to imagine such an enlightened being and even harder for us to aim for such enlightenment. More discouraging still is the quality of public life today, the low level of discourse and the presence of so much ego, anger, greed, jealousy, spite, cruelty, lust, fear, anxiety and turmoil! I felt a new determination dawning inside me.

In this my most important decision I decided to help discover the nature of India's true self in its children. My own work and indeed I as a person were relegated to the background. My scientific career, my teams, my awards, all this became secondary. I wanted instead to be a part of the eternal intelligence that is India. I hoped to transcend myself and discover the inner, higher self that is in us through my interaction with joyous children.

A man is said to pass through different stages in his lifetime. Dr Wayne W. Dyer, in his book *Manifest Your Destiny*, makes an interesting categorization of them as athelete stage, warrior stage, statesperson stage and spirit stage. It occurred to me that nations too make a similar transition and in extending this analogy to them I have termed the last two stages big brother and self-realization stages respectively. The stages do not follow in sequence necessarily; they can be coexistent, with one aspect dominant.

In the first, athlete stage, a nation fresh from an independence struggle, or some other transition, embarks on an energetic pursuit of performance and achievement. This has happened in Japan, Singapore and Malaysia.

When a nation leaves this stage behind, it generally enters the warrior stage. Proud of its achievements, it finds ways to demonstrate its superiority over others, perhaps through conquest. Ego is the driving force. During this stage people are busy with goals and achievements in competition with others and this, as Dyer points out for the individual, generates anxiety. Convincing others of its superiority becomes the theme.

In the next, big brother stage, the ego has been tamed somewhat and with its newfound maturity awareness shifts to what is important to other nations and societies. In the big brother stage the nation is still an achiever but it is not so obsessed with proving its strength. The idea is to help others become better. The erstwhile Soviet Union by its developmental role in some countries had adopted this role. As with the individual, so too with the nation, the transition from the warrior stage to the big brother stage is a rewarding but difficult exercise.

11

There is one stage even higher than this big brother stage. In this, a nation recognizes its truest essence. It comes out of the wisdom that the earth is no single nation's inheritance but of all, and its people are aware of the responsibility of the individual towards his fellow human beings. This can be called the realization stage, and India may have the potential to achieve it.

In my working career of forty-three years, I have changed my tasks in several institutions. Change is crucial. It brings new thought; new thought leads to innovative actions. On 15 August 2001, I took a decision to go for another change. I mentioned my intention to Prime Minister Atal Bihari Vajpayee, who asked me to rethink. I had spoken to him of my desire to be relieved on a few earlier occasions too but he advised me to continue and prevailed.

As a rocket man too I worked with stages. Each stage is jettisoned after taking the rocket further along its intended trajectory. I worked with the Indian Space Research Organization (ISRO) during 1963–82. In 1980, India launched its first satellite launch vehicle successfully that put the Rohini satellite into orbit and became a member of the exclusive space club. I headed the team as Project Director of the mission for SLV-3. Our success in this effort gave the nation satellite launch vehicle technology and expertise in control, guidance, propulsion and aerodynamics, besides the ability to design various rocket systems. Above all, this project enriched the organization with enhanced capabilities in design, development and management systems integrating inputs from different institutions such as R&D laboratories, industry and academia. And the programme also gave leaders in technology and management. Today they are all working in various space and defence programmes. This was my first stage, in which I learnt leadership from three great teachers—Dr Vikram Sarabhai, Prof. Satish Dhawan and Dr Brahm Prakash. This was the time of learning and acquisition of knowledge for me.

The second stage could then be from 1982 in the Defence Research and Development Organization (DRDO). Again it was teamwork against the background of denial of technology through the instruments of the Missile Technology Control

Regime (MTCR) and the Nuclear Non-Proliferation Treaty (NPT). I had the opportunity to work with teams and DRDO labs that led to the design, development, production and operationalization of two strategic missiles. These types of strategic missiles will not be available to India from any country, no matter how friendly our relations with it. During this period, three new laboratories and facilities, one in the area of missile technology called Research Centre Imarat (RCI) at Hyderabad and two other missile test centres, one on the mainland and the other on an island, near Chandipur on the coast of Bay of Bengal, were born with excellent capabilities. In addition, the nation became strong as capability in critical technologies emerged from laboratories and academic institutions that helped us overcome the constraints of the MTCR. My team could design and develop any type of missile system, including the Intercontinental Ballistic Missile (ICBM).

During this stage, I have gone through many successes and some failures. I learnt from failures and hardened myself with courage to face them. This was my second stage, which taught me the crucial lesson of managing failures.

The third stage can be the participation in India's mission to become a nuclear-weapon state with a great partnership between the Department of Atomic Energy (DAE) and DRDO with the support of the armed forces. This was a mission well accomplished.

However, when children ask me, 'What has given you happiness in your life in the last forty years?' I say I get happiness when heart patients carry KR coronary stent in their arteries and when the physically handicapped children fitted with the lightweight Floor Reaction Orthosis (FRO) callipers find their difficulties eased somewhat. Both of these came as spin-offs from missile technologies.

During this stage, I held the position of Chairman of the Technology Information, Forecasting and Assessment Council (TIFAC) under the Department of Science and Technology, for nearly two tenures (about eight years). This period saw the creation of Technology Vision 2020 based on the work of task teams consisting of 500 experts in all who had available to them inputs from 5,000 scientists and technologists from different fields. Later, the Technology Vision document and the national security aspects got integrated and the India Millennium Missions (IMM 2020) emerged. When I took over as Principal Scientific Adviser to the Government of India, in November 1999, the task was to do detailing and evolve a working plan for IMM 2020. It is indeed a roadmap for transforming India into a developed country—the Second Vision of the Nation. Certain experimental work on education, agriculture and also development of a number of villages in an integrated way is currently progressing. A Cabinet paper on the subject has been moved for approval of the government. During this third stage, it was building technological strength with institutional partnership, adapting technology to societal needs and formulating the vision for the Nation that occupied me.

The helicopter mishap of 30 September 2001 made me realize that the time to jettison the third stage had arrived. This thought was further reinforced on 2 October, the birthday of Mahatma Gandhi, when I visited Mata Amritanandamayi's Ashram at Kollam in Kerala. She emphasized the need to integrate spirituality with education to create a new generation of leaders and entrepreneurs. On 12 October 2001, three days before I would complete my seventy orbits around the sun, I formally wrote to the Prime Minister about my decision to retire and requested to be relieved in a month's time. He relented this time and I prevailed.

Meanwhile I keep visiting schools. During my visits to many states, particularly two of the north-eastern states, Assam and Tripura, and Jharkhand and also a few places in Tamil Nadu, I have addressed thousands of students, about 40,000 at last count. I have found that I communicate well with this age group; I share their imagination. Most important, through my interaction with them, I feel I can ignite in their minds a love for science, and through it, a sense of mission for achieving a developed India.

Will this be my fourth stage? Shall I be successful? I really don't know. But what I do know is that there is no greater power in heaven or on earth than the commitment to a dream. Dreams hold something of that energy which lies at the heart of all things and are the binding force that brings the spiritual and the material together.

It had been in my mind for the past few years to undertake research and teaching. For this purpose, combined with my desire to find time to meet schoolchildren, I have shifted to Anna University—my alma mater. What a great feeling it is to be among young people bubbling with creativity and enthusiasm! What a great responsibility the elders of this country have at hand to guide this tremendous energy in a constructive way for nation building! How can we make up for missed opportunities and the failures of the past?

Summary

Spirituality must be integrated with education. Self-realization is the focus. Each one of us must become aware of our higher self. We are links of a great past to a grand future. We should ignite our dormant inner energy and let it guide our lives. The radiance of such minds embarked on constructive endeavour will bring peace, prosperity and bliss to this nation.

2

GIVE US A ROLE MODEL

Men often become what they believe themselves to
be. If I believe I cannot do something, it makes me
incapable of doing it. But when I believe I can, then
I acquire the ability to do it even if I didn't have it in
the beginning.

—Mahatma Gandhi

Why should I meet young students in particular? Seeking
the answer I went back to my student days. From the
island of Rameswaram, what a great journey it's been!
Looking back it all seems quite incredible. What was
it that made it possible? Hard work? Ambition? Many

things come to my mind. I feel the most important thing was that I always assessed my worth by the value of my contribution. The fundamental thing is that you must know that you deserve the good things of life, the benefits that God bestows. Unless our students and young believe that they are worthy of being citizens of a developed India, how will they ever be responsible and enlightened citizens?

There is nothing mysterious about the abundance in developed nations. The historic fact is that the people of these nations—the G8 as they are called—believed over many generations that they must live a good life in a strong and prosperous nation. The reality became aligned with their aspirations.

I do not think that abundance and spirituality are mutually exclusive or that it is wrong to desire material things. For instance, while I personally cherish a life with minimum of possessions, I admire abundance, for it brings along with it security and confidence, and these eventually help preserve our freedom. Nature too does not do anything by half measures, as you will see if you look around you. Go to a garden. In season, there is a profusion of flowers. Or look up. The universe stretches into infinitude, vast beyond belief.

All that we see in the world is an embodiment of energy. We are a part of the cosmic energy too, as Sri Aurobindo says. Therefore when we begin to appreciate that spirit and matter are both part of existence, are in harmony with each other, we shall realize that it is wrong to feel that it is somehow shameful or non-spiritual to desire material things.

Yet, this is what we are often led to believe. Certainly there is nothing wrong with an attitude of making do with the minimum, in leading a life of asceticism. Mahatma Gandhi led such a life but in his case as in yours it has to be a matter of choice. You follow such a lifestyle because it answers a need that arises from deep within you. However, making a virtue of sacrifice and what is forced upon you—to celebrate suffering—is a different thing altogether. This was the basis of my decision to contact our young. To know their dreams and tell them that it is perfectly all right to dream of a good life, an abundant life, a life full of pleasures and comforts, and work for that golden era.

Whatever you do must come from the heart, express your spirit, and thereby you will also spread love and joy around you.

My first such meeting took place in a high school in Tripura. It was a gathering of 500 students and teachers. After my talk on the second vision for transforming India into a developed nation, there were a series of questions, two of which I would like to discuss. The first question was: 'Where do we get a role model from, how do you get a role model?'

Whether we are aware of it or not, from childhood onwards, through various phases of life, we adopt role models. I said, 'When you are growing up, say till the age of fifteen, the best role model I can think of would be your father, your mother and your schoolteacher.' They, to my mind, are the people who can impart the best guidance during this period. I turned to the teachers and parents present there and told them what a big responsibility they have. I personally believe the full development of a child with a value system can only come from these people. In my own home, when I was growing up, I used to see my father and mother say namaz five times a day, and in spite of their modest financial resources, I found them always giving to the needy around. My teacher, Sivasubramania Iyer, was responsible for persuading my father to send me to school setting aside financial constraints. It is very important for every parent to be willing to make the effort to guide children to be good human beings—enlightened and hard-working. The teacher, the child's window to learning and knowledge, has to play the role model in generating creativity in the child. This triangle is indeed the real role model I can think of. I would even go to the extent of saying that if parents and teachers show the required dedication to shape the lives of the young, India would get a new life. As it is said: Behind the parents stands the school, and behind the teacher the home. Education and the teacher-student relationship have to be seen not in business terms but with the nation's growth in mind. A proper education would help nurture a sense of dignity and self-respect among our youth. These are qualities no law can enforce—they have to be nurtured ourselves.

The children enjoyed this answer though I don't know whether the parents and teachers got the message.

Another girl in all seriousness asked, 'Every day we read in the newspaper or hear our parents talk about atankvadis (terrorists). Who are they? Do they belong to our country?' This question really shocked me. I myself was searching for an answer. They are our own people. Sometimes we create them through political and economic isolation. Or they can be fanatics, sometimes sponsored by hostile nations, trying to disrupt normal life through terrorism. I looked at the audience, at the people sitting by my side, at the teachers, and at the sky for an answer. I said, 'Children, I am reminded of our epics, the Ramayana and Mahabharata. In the Ramayana the battle is between the divine hero Rama and demon king Ravana. It is a long-drawn battle that finally Rama wins. In the Mahabharata, there is the battle at Kurukshetra. In this fight between good and evil, Dharma wins again. The battles are many but finally peace triumphs. In our times too we have seen this battle between good and evil—for instance, the

Second World War. It seems to me that both good and evil will survive side by side. The Almighty does help them both to various degrees! How to minimize the evil through our spiritual growth is a question that has persisted throughout human history.'

On another occasion, I addressed a very large gathering of students at St Mary's School, Dindigul in Tamil Nadu on their seventy-fifth anniversary celebrations. Among the large number of children wishing to meet me were two who were in a hurry to get an answer from me. One student asked, 'I have read your book *Agni Siragugal* (the Tamil version of *Wings of Fire*). You always give a message to dream. Tell me, why dream?'

My answer was to ask the gathered children to recite the following: 'Dream, dream, dream. Dream transforms into thoughts. Thoughts result in actions.' I told them, 'Friends, if there are no dreams, there are no revolutionary thoughts; if there are no thoughts, no actions will emanate. Hence, parents and teachers should allow their children to dream. Success always follows dreams attempted though there may be some setbacks and delays.'

Another boy asked, 'Please tell me, who would be the first scientist in the world?' It occurred to me— science was born and survives only by questions. The whole foundation of science is questioning. And as parents and teachers well know, children are the source of unending questions. Hence, 'Child is the first scientist,' I replied. There was thunderous applause. The children enjoyed this different way of thinking. Teachers and parents also smiled at the answer.

During my visit to Assam, I visited Tezpur. I had gone for the convocation ceremony of Tezpur University and also to receive the honorary doctorate conferred on me. After the convocation, I took off to meet schoolchildren. It was a big gathering of young people. The theme of my address was 'Indomitable Spirit'. As soon as I finished my talk the youngsters mobbed me for autographs. When I finished giving autographs I faced two interesting questions. One was: 'Why cannot water from the Brahmaputra, which is in flood much of the time, be diverted to Rajasthan or Tamil Nadu which are starved of water?'

Only children will have these innovative ideas. Grown-ups tend to see more impossibilities. It was such a powerful question, I was completely beaten. I was sure even the Prime Minister would not have been able to answer it! How to tell the boy, rivers are a state subject and our states are fighting for the rights to their waters? That these would bring them prosperity some day but meanwhile they were flowing wastefully into the sea and causing floods every year. How to answer it?

I said, 'India Vision 2020 demands from the young that they start a great mission of connecting rivers cutting across the states.' I personally feel the young have the most powerful minds. They can overcome the negativity of the bureaucracy and some self-centred policies of the state governments to enrich the people of the country. They can even improve coordination between the states and the Centre. And they surely will!

Another student asked me a question for which again I had no ready answer. He said, 'Sir, big leaders in any field don't come and talk to us. We see our

Prime Minister often going to Chennai, Lucknow, and many places. But he never comes here. We want him; we want to talk to him.' I was impressed by this urge to communicate with the country's leaders. I said, when I reach Delhi, I will tell your dream to the leaders and your dream will come true.

I later narrated this to the Prime Minister. He conceded the point and said, 'Children don't talk to me any more. Maybe the security cordon has created a separation.' I request our leaders in different fields to interact more with the children of the country for a better understanding of their own purpose in life as also for helping create a better future for our children.

I have visited Jharkhand a number of times after its formation. Every time I visit it, I am struck by the tremendous resources that wait to be harnessed in the state, which will multiply its wealth manifold. At the Sri Ramakrishna High School, Bokaro, I addressed a gathering of about 3,000 students and saw their creativity on display in an exhibition of their paintings, toys and other items made by them. In my conversation with them, one student asked me, 'In Jharkhand, it is green everywhere. We have forests, streams and hills. Why is it that we have a desert in Rajasthan?'

The question reminded me of a similar one in Assam: Why cannot the Brahmaputra's waters be taken to Tamil Nadu and Rajasthan? 'You know, twenty years ago, you would not have seen much cultivation in Rajasthan. But once the Indira Gandhi Canal was constructed agriculture became possible in many places. It is possible for man to transform the desert into a fertile land.' I repeated what I had told the student in Assam. 'It has to be one of the greatest missions of India to connect rivers so that water can reach many water-starved states. Visionary action is needed. When you grow up you will probably be part of reconstructing this nation and giving shape to these thoughts.'

One child came to me with a serious expression and asked, 'Sir, will your Agni missile cross the ocean and reach America?'

I was a little startled by this thought. 'For us no country is our enemy to send Agni there. Particularly America is our friend. Agni symbolizes our strength. It shows that India has all the capabilities.'

During my visit to Cuttack I participated in the birthday celebrations of the late Justice Harihar Mahapatra. I went there at the invitation of Justice Ranganath Mishra. For me, it was a revelation, how the independence movement, the first vision for the nation, had created the larger-than-life figure of Justice Harihar Mahapatra. He lived to the age of ninety-two and established Cuttack Eye Hospital, Utkal University and above all organized multi-pronged efforts to remove poverty. My biography in Oriya was released. At the end of my speech the youngsters crowding around put forth many questions.

The first question was, 'Sir, tell us which are your favourite books, that you loved and which have shaped your mind?'

I said, 'Four books in my life have been very close to my heart. I cherish reading them. The first is *Man the Unknown* by Dr Alexis Carrel, a doctor-turned-philosopher and a Nobel laureate. This book highlights how the mind and body both have to be treated in an ailment as the two are integrated. You cannot treat one and ignore the other. In particular, children who dream of becoming doctors should read the book. They will learn that the human body is not a mechanical system; it is a very intelligent organism with a most intricate and sensitive feedback system. The second book, one I venerate, is Tiruvalluvar's *Thirukkural,* which provides an excellent code of life. The third is *Light from Many Lamps* by Lillian Eichler Watson which has touched me deeply. It illuminates how we live and has been an invaluable guide to me for fifty years. And the Holy Quran is, of course, a constant companion.'

While I was addressing another gathering of schoolchildren in Anand, Gujarat, one smart boy asked a very intelligent question: 'Who is our enemy?' I liked the question and put it to the other students, encouraging them to come forward with their views. Then came the answer, 'Poverty.' What a wise reaction from this young child whom I have mentioned in the dedication.

The last question, which I am including here, came from the powerful mind of another child. 'Tell me, sir, are Pakistani weapons stronger than Indian ones?' I asked the child why this doubt arose in his mind. Reports he read in the media led him to think so, he said.

'This is a unique characteristic of our country—to belittle our capabilities. It may even be genetic!' I said. 'India can design, develop and produce any type of missile and any type of nuclear weapon. This is a capability only four countries in the world have. You remove all the doubts from your mind,' I told the child, who gave me a very satisfied look.

I have selected only eleven questions here from among the hundreds of questions I have been asked during the course of meeting 40,000 high school students so far. The questions reflect the children's innocence, but most of all they show how strongly they feel the desire to live in a strong and prosperous nation. I also realized from these sessions how important it is for them to have role models, whether in science, industry, sports, entertainment or some other field. The question is: Can we give our children a role model? And how?

At the dawn of the new millennium came the news that the human genome had been decoded.

All the 30,000 genes that human beings carry today, we are told, are identical to those of our Stone Age ancestors who lived thousands of years ago. One of the traits that has come down to us from them, along with others that are needed for survival, is the desire for achievement.

It is said that nature gave us this instinct because the need to achieve, like the need to reproduce, the need to eat, the need to drink and the need to breathe, is simply too important to be left to chance. History shows the hunger for achievement is a highly evolved one and undoubtedly the strongest one. We tend to forget it but it underlines much of our experience. Most important, without it, how would we learn and grow, aspire to greater perfection?

I have seen Dr Vikram Sarabhai's vision succeeding over three decades through sustained and coordinated achievement. At work in that and any other endeavour was this same desire to exceed the limits. As we try and excel, role models play a guiding role. The power of Vikram Sarabhai was such that others took up his vision and completed it long after he was no more. For you it could be someone else whom you admire—a sportsperson, a teacher, a successful entrepreneur.

I recently had the chance to meet a legendary personality, a role model herself. Lata Mangeshkar was presiding over a function in remembrance of her father, Master Deenanath Mangeshkar. Lata Mangeshkar is a recipient of the Bharat Ratna and I felt honoured that she had asked me to inaugurate the 450-bed Deenanath Hospital and Research Centre in Pune. I visited the hospital just before the inauguration. I found that it would be treating nearly 30 per cent of the patients free. I was touched by the fact that despite her wealth and fame, she had not lost sight of the fact that one needs to do all one can to help relieve the suffering of others.

Her songs played over the radio have brought pleasure to countless hearts over the decades. During the India–China conflict in 1962, her song 'Ae mere vatan ke logo' moved an entire nation. Few people can claim to have influenced the lives of millions in such a delightful way.

Role models can help us focus on what is correct for us as individuals, as groups and, of course, as a nation. They can also lead us to great success. We seem to have got carried away with the success of a few in the field of information technology. But that is indeed nothing compared to what we can and should achieve. Ancient India was a knowledge society and a leader in many intellectual pursuits, particularly in the fields of mathematics, medicine and astronomy. A renaissance is imperative for us to once again become a knowledge superpower rather than simply providing cheap labour in areas of high technology.

Summary

A nation's wealth is the young generation of the country. When they grow up, who can be the role models? Mother, father and elementary schoolteachers play a very important part as role models. When the child grows up, the role models will be national leaders of quality and integrity in every field including politics, the sciences, technology and industry.

35

3

VISIONARY TEACHERS AND SCIENTISTS

Whatever you can do or dream you can, begin it.
Boldness has genius, power and magic in it. Begin
it now.

—Goethe

The great minds of the country had the ability to make others join their endeavour to convert dreams into reality. For them, the nation was bigger than themselves and they could draw thousands to act upon their dreams.

In December 2000, I had participated in the birth centenary celebrations of Adhyapaka Rathna

T. Totadri Iyengar. I graduated in science from St Joseph's College, Tiruchirapalli (1954). As a young student I saw Prof. T. Totadri Iyengar—a unique, divine-looking personality—walking through the college campus every morning and teaching mathematics to the students of B.Sc. (Honours) and M.Sc. The students looked at him with awe as one would at a guru, which indeed he was. When he walked, knowledge radiated all around. At that time, 'Calculus' Srinivasan was my mathematics teacher. He used to talk about Prof. Totadri Iyengar with deep respect and would organize integrated classes for first year B.Sc. (Honours) and first year B.Sc. (Physics) to be taught by him. I also had the opportunity to attend some of these classes, particularly on the subjects of modern algebra and statistics. When we were in first year B.Sc., 'Calculus' Srinivasan used to pick the top ten students as members of the Mathematics Club of St Joseph's where Prof. Totadri Iyengar used to give a lecture series.

One day, in 1952, he gave a lecture on ancient mathematicians and astronomers of India. He spoke for nearly one hour. The lecture still rings in my ears. Let me share with you my thoughts about some ancient mathematicians, glimpses of whom I saw in Prof. Totadri Iyengar in my own way.

Aryabhata, born in AD 476 in Kusumapura (now called Patna), was an astronomer and mathematician. He was reputed to be a repository of all the mathematical knowledge known at that point of time. He was only twenty-three years old when he wrote *Aryabhatiyam* in two parts. The text covers arithmetic, algebra and trigonometry and, of course, astronomy. He gave formulae for the areas of a triangle and a circle and attempted to give the volumes of a sphere and a pyramid. He was the first to give an approximation to pi as the ratio of a circle's circumference and diameter, arriving at the value of 3.1416. To celebrate this great astronomer, India named its first satellite launched in 1975 Aryabhata.

Brahmagupta was born in AD 598 at Billamala in Rajasthan in the empire of Harsha. He wrote the *Brahma Sphuta Siddhanta* at the age of thirty. He updated works of astronomy. He covered progressions and geometry. He also studied and gave what is known as the solution of indeterminate equations of different degrees as well as solutions to quadratic equations.

Bhaskaracharya was another unique intellectual of his time. He was born in AD 1114 at Vijjalbada, located at what is now the border of Karnataka and Maharashtra. He wrote the famous *Siddhanthasiromani* in four chapters. He dealt with astronomy and algebra and is known to be the first recognized mathematician who evolved value to zero from the concept based on Aryabhata's discovery. To honour him, ISRO's second series of satellites was named Bhaskara I and II (1979 and 1981).

The work of these three mathematicians of India provides the context of Albert Einstein's remark that 'We owe a lot to the Indians who taught us how to count, without which no worthwhile scientific discovery could have been made.'

Then comes to my mind the greatest of all geniuses ever known and acknowledged, and who lived within our present memory—Srinivasa Ramanujan. He lived only for thirty-three years (1887–1920) and had no practical formal education or means of living. Yet, his inexhaustible spirit and love for his subject enabled him to make a vast contribution to mathematical research and some of his contributions are still under serious study, engaging the efforts of mathematicians to establish formal proofs. Ramanujan was a unique Indian genius who could melt the heart of as rigorous a mathematician as Prof. G.H. Hardy of Trinity College, Cambridge. In fact, it is not an exaggeration to say that it was Hardy who discovered Ramanujan for the world. Why do not our reputed scientists locate another Ramanujan in our schools? Oh my friends why don't you in every field integrate and grow instead of differentiating!

'Every integer is a personal friend of Ramanujan,' one of the tributes to Ramanujan said and it was no exaggeration. Prof. Hardy, while rating geniuses on a scale of 100, put most of them in the range of around 30, giving a rating of 60 to the rare exception. However, for Ramanujan, he suggested, only the value of 100 would fit. There can be no better tribute to either Ramanujan or to the Indian heritage. Ramanujan's work covers vast areas including prime numbers, hyper geometric series, modular functions, elliptic functions, mock theta functions, even magic squares, apart from some serious work on the geometry of ellipses, squaring the circle and so on.

I hope that eminent teachers who teach and inspire the young students of mathematics will continue their unmatched and noble services in the years to come, thus ensuring the march of Indian brilliance in this field. Prof. S. Chandrasekhar, the astrophysicist, continued the Indian mathematics tradition in his work abroad. Of course mathematics is universal. Now the tradition will further blossom with the efforts of Prof. C.S. Seshadri, Prof. J.V. Narlikar, Prof. M.S. Narasimhan, Prof. S.R.S. Varadhan, Prof. M.S. Raghunathan, Prof. Narender Karmakar and Prof. Ashok Sen, among others.

Sir C.V. Raman started his career in the Office of the Accountant General, Calcutta. But the scientist in him would not let him rest and he was always probing for answers to some of the problems that interested him. Fortunately, he was supported by the great educationist

Ashutosh Mukherjee, who encouraged Sir C.V. Raman to pursue his research. It is noteworthy that the Raman Effect, the discovery of which brought him the Nobel Prize, did not come out of a grand establishment set up at vast expense. I believe the urge to show to the world the excellence of Indian minds would have been a major motivating factor for Sir C.V. Raman. The same is the case with Prof. S. Chandrasekhar, also a Nobel laureate for his work on black holes. There are some interesting statements in his biography *Chandra* by Kameshwar C. Wali. As it points out, 'Chandra grew up in what was a golden age for science, art and literature in India, spurred on partly by the struggle for independence. J.C. Bose, C.V. Raman, Meghnad Saha, Srinivasa Ramanujan, and Rabindranath Tagore, by their achievements in scientific and creative endeavours, became national heroes along with Jawaharlal Nehru, Mahatma Gandhi, and a host of others . . .' Possibly, their great success helped produce an atmosphere of creativity. Howsoever it may be, it is worth noting, as Chandrasekhar observed, 'that in the modern era before 1910, there were no (Indian) scientists of international reputation or standing. Between 1920 and 1925, we had suddenly five or six internationally well-known men. I myself have associated this remarkable phenomenon with the need for self-expression, which became a dominant motive among the young during the national movement. It was a part of the national movement to assert oneself. India was a subject country, but . . . particularly in science, we could show the West in their own realm that we were equal to them'.

Here I would like to quote Sir C.V. Raman, who said in 1969 while addressing young graduates, 'I would like to tell the young men and women before me not to lose hope and courage. Success can only come to you by courageous devotion to the task lying in front of you. I can assert without fear of contradiction that the quality of the Indian mind is equal to the quality of any Teutonic, Nordic or Anglo-Saxon mind. What we lack is perhaps courage, what we lack is perhaps driving force, which takes one anywhere. We have, I think, developed an inferiority complex. I think what is needed in India today is the destruction of that defeatist spirit. We need a spirit of victory, a spirit that will carry us to our rightful place under the sun, a spirit which can recognize that we, as inheritors of a proud civilization, are entitled to our rightful place on this planet. If that indomitable spirit were to arise nothing can hold us from achieving our rightful destiny.'

Further afield, there was similarly the emergence of others who were great in their respective fields. Interestingly, a music trinity of great saints, Thiagaraja Swamigal, Muthuswamy Deekshidar and Shyama Sastrigal, also emerged at the same time in south India within a 50-km radius. What we should note is that the movement for independence generated the best of leaders in arts, science, technology, economics, history and literature who stand with the best in the world.

In more recent times too we have seen the emergence of great visionary scientists. Particularly, I was interested in the lives of three scientists—Dr D.S. Kothari, Dr Homi J. Bhabha and Dr Vikram Sarabhai. I wanted to learn more about their leadership qualities in the scientific and technological fields which helped link these to the development of the nation. They are the founders of three great institutions—DRDO, DAE, ISRO.

Dr D.S. Kothari, a professor at Delhi University, was an outstanding physicist and astrophysicist. He is well known for ionization of matter by pressure in cold compact objects like planets. This theory is complementary to the epoch-making theory of thermal ionization of his guru, Dr Meghnad Saha. Dr D.S. Kothari set a scientific tradition in Indian defence tasks when he became Scientific Adviser to Defence Minister in 1948. The first thing he did was to establish the Defence Science Centre to do research in electronic materials, nuclear medicine and ballistic science. He is considered the architect of defence science in India. We are celebrating this great mind through a research chair at the Indian Institute of Science.

Dr Bhabha did research in theoretical physics at Cambridge University. From 1930 to 1939, Homi Bhabha carried out research relating to cosmic radiation. In 1939, he joined Sir C.V. Raman at IISc, Bangalore. Later, he founded the Tata Institute of Fundamental Research with focus on nuclear and mathematical sciences. He established the Atomic Energy Commission in 1948. His vision led to the setting up of numerous centres in the field of nuclear science and technology, such as those for producing nuclear power, or for research in nuclear medicine. These science institutions generated further technological centres keeping nuclear science as the vital component.

Dr Sarabhai, the youngest of the three, had worked with Sir C.V. Raman in experimental cosmic rays. He established the Physical Research Laboratory at Ahmedabad with space research as the focus. In 1963, Thumba Equatorial Rocket Launching Station (TERLS) began launching sounding rockets for atmospheric research. Dr Sarabhai established the Space Science & Technology Centre (SSTC) and was its director. His vision led to the establishment of ISRO with its allied centres responsible for development of launch vehicles, satellites, mission management and applications.

These three Indian scientists, all of them physicists, started physics research institutions that blossomed into defence technology, nuclear technology and space technology, which now employ 20,000 scientists in centres spread around the country. One thing I noted was that all three realized the importance of making the political leadership understand what science could do for the country. It is essential that technologies that give immediate benefits to the people be taken up for implementation by the system regardless of which party is in power. Another important message conveyed by these scientists is that basic science is vital for growth of technology and for developing new leaders in science. Let us learn from them the proven qualities of leadership to value science and technology in an integrated way.

In 1962, Dr Sarabhai and Dr Bhabha were looking for a site to establish the space research station in the equatorial region. Thumba in Kerala was found most suitable as it was near the equatorial region and was ideally suited for ionospheric research. The locality, however, was inhabited by thousands of fishermen living in the villages there. It also had a beautiful church called St Mary Magdalene Church and the

Bishop's house. As such, the acquisition of the land did not move any further.

Dr Sarabhai met the Bishop, His Excellency Rev. Dr Peter Bernard Pereira, on a Saturday and requested transfer of the property. The Bishop smiled and asked him to meet him the next day. In the Sunday morning service, the Bishop told the congregation, 'My children, I have a famous scientist with me who wants our church and the place I live for the work of space science and research. Science seeks truth that enriches human life. The higher level of religion is spirituality. The spiritual preachers seek the help of the Almighty to bring peace to human minds. In short, what Vikram is doing and what I am doing are the same—both science and spirituality seek the Almighty's blessings for human prosperity in mind and body. Children, can we give them God's abode for a scientific mission?' There was silence for a while followed by a hearty 'Amen' from the congregation which made the whole church reverberate.

It was indeed a great experience working with Dr Sarabhai from 1963 to 1971. As a young engineer engaged in the tasks of composite technology, explosive systems and rocket engineering systems at the Thiruvananthapuram space centre I drew tremendous energy from his leadership. Though the nation was in its technological infancy, Dr Sarabhai was dreaming of developing our own satellite launch vehicles. These would be used to launch from Indian soil remote sensing satellites in sun-synchronous orbit and communication satellites in geosynchronous orbit. Today, his vision is almost realized with the launch of the Geosynchronous Launch Vehicle (GSLV). ISRO has also operationalized the IRS and INSAT systems, thereby bringing the benefits of space to the common man.

There is an experience I would like to share with you in relation to Dr Sarabhai's vision for space programmes. I wrote briefly in *Wings of Fire* about this episode. The design project of India's first satellite launch vehicle (SLV-3) was taken up at the Vikram Sarabhai Space Centre (VSSC). The design of each stage of rocket, heat shield and guidance system was given to selected project leaders. I was given the design project of the fourth stage of SLV-3, that is, the upper stage rocket, which would give the final velocity to put Rohini into orbit. This fourth stage uses an advanced composite material that provides high strength with minimum weight. It also has maximum loading of high energy solid propellant. While we were developing the design of this upper stage in 1970, I received a call from Dr Sarabhai from Ahmedabad stating that he would be visiting Thiruvananthapuram along with Prof. Hubert Curien, chairman of CNES, the French space agency. I was asked to give a presentation about the fourth stage to Prof. Curien's team. When the presentation was over, we realized that the SLV-3 fourth stage was also being considered as upper stage for the French Diamont P-4 launch vehicle. The CNES needed an apogee rocket motor nearly double the propellant weight and also size of the stage that we had designed.

A decision was then taken in the same meeting that the fourth stage should be reconfigured to match and suit both Diamont P-4 and SLV-3. I mention this episode because at the time this decision was taken, we ourselves were in the design stage! Such was Dr Sarabhai's confidence in the Indian scientific community. Development work on this stage started ahead of the other stages of SLV-3. With our motivation thus boosted, work proceeded in full swing. A series of reviews took place between the two teams and the fourth stage graduated from drawing board to developing stage. Unfortunately in 1971, Dr Sarabhai passed away, and at the same time the French government called off the Diamont P-4 programme.

Once the fourth stage was developed and a series of tests was going on, a new requirement appeared on the horizon, in the form of India building a small communication satellite to be launched by the European Ariane launch vehicle. For the APPLE—Ariane Passenger Payload Experiment—communication satellite, the SLV-3 fourth stage proved a perfect fit and it was included in the payload of the Ariane launch in 1981 from Kourou, French Guiana. The vision seeded in 1970 by Dr Vikram Sarabhai was indeed realized when APPLE was placed in geostationary orbit and started communicating with our earth stations. APPLE's success proved that a vision with committed scientific support will achieve its aim. This achievement came as a fantastic fillip to the rocket technologists in the country. The visionary may not be with us today but his vision gets realized.

The dream of Dr Sarabhai was shaped into reality by Prof. Satish Dhawan. After he took charge of ISRO from 1972, Prof. Dhawan structured and nurtured ISRO with a space profile and his work led to many significant accomplishments and benefits from a number of remote sensing and communication satellites. The Polar Satellite Launch Vehicle accomplished the feat of launching multiple satellites for India and other countries, injecting them in different orbits in a single mission.

I learned an important lesson in management from Prof. Dhawan when I was appointed Project Director SLV-3 in 1972 to design, develop and launch the first satellite launch vehicle to inject Rohini into near earth orbit. This was that when a Project Director is appointed, the whole organization—including the Chairman ISRO—works for his success. It is a lesson that has been of abiding value all through the other projects I have worked on. The other thing I have learnt after more than forty years of working in three departments in various projects and programmes is that you will succeed as a project leader as long as you remember that the project is bigger than you. Wherever the project leader tries to make himself out to be bigger than the project, the enterprise suffers.

I recall my working at ISRO Headquarters, Bangalore, as Director, Launch Vehicle Programmes/ Systems, in the early 1980s, when we were debating the performance and cost-effectiveness of launch vehicles. In 1981, the scientists of VSSC, Thiruvananthapuram, with the help of other ISRO centres, evolved a configuration of the PSLV core vehicle with two large strap-on boosters. The PSLV weighed about 400 tonnes at take-off. Prof. Dhawan wanted to study an alternative and simple configuration. I and some of my colleagues, A. Sivathanu Pillai, N. Sundararajan and K. Padmanabha Menon, carried out mission, technology and feasibility studies for the optimal configuration. The team designed several options, including a unique core vehicle with an advanced solid propellant booster, using first stage rockets of SLV-3 as strap-ons. This brought the PSLV weight down to only about 275 tonnes at take-off. Prof. Dhawan used to come almost daily to my small room, which was close to his office, and debate the possible configuration choice. He was himself a foremost aerodynamic specialist with mathematics and system engineering background, and would illustrate his ideas on the blackboard and ask us to do more homework. We also studied the growth opportunities of PSLV with cryogenic upper stage as a GSLV and the possibility of launching due-east geosynchronous missions. Prof. Dhawan put the two most favoured configurations up for discussion among the experts and the ISRO teams. Detailed examination and debate, taking the long-term plans into account, took place and they chose the PSLV configuration as proposed by my launch vehicle team. Prof. Dhawan considered the future scenario of operationalization of PSLV and GSLV, bearing in mind the satellites and application programmes, and decided on this unique configuration and evolved the roadmap for ISRO for the next fifteen years. I and Prof. Narasimha brought out a book, *Development in Fluid Mechanics and Space Technology*, with Prof. Dhawan's handwritten fifteen-year space profile, based on the chosen PSLV configuration.

A memorable day for me is 31 May 1982. Prof. Dhawan gave me a send-off in an unconventional way. He called an ISRO council meeting to discuss the future launch vehicle programme. I made a presentation to the directors of the ISRO centres on performance and cost-effectiveness of our launch vehicles and the growth profile. After the presentation, Prof. Dhawan broke the news that he had given me to DRDO. This decision indeed gave me a change that led to progress in a different field.

We see today self-reliance in launch vehicle technology with PSLV operational and GSLV getting ready to be operationalized. This is close to the direction envisaged in the early 1980s by Prof. Dhawan. The recognition of ISRO as a successful organization was due to the strong foundation and space profile envisioned by him. One test of leadership is also how well successors are able to carry forward a programme. At ISRO, Prof. U.R. Rao and Dr K. Kasturirangan brought further success and glory to the organization. After his retirement Prof. Dhawan continued as a member of the Space Commission and in that capacity continued to help the organization which he built. Remarkably, Prof. Dhawan saw the space missions envisioned by him come into being in his lifetime. He also saw in his lifetime many of those he had tutored emerge as strong technology leaders themselves who have contributed immeasurably to the country. What a great personality he was!

After joining the DRDO, I started the missile development programme there. During the Integrated Guided Missile Development Programme (IGMDP), the focus was to design missiles with state-of-the-art performance at the time of deployment. The surface-to-surface missile Prithvi became the best in its class and users' delight with its high accuracy, reliable performance and the manoeuvrable trajectories. The first stage of SLV-3 became handy to configure Agni as a long-range deterrent. It blossomed from the

REX (Re-Entry eXperiment) programme conceived by my team in 1981. Both Prithvi and Agni are in production and induction phase. Trishul, which is a surface-to-air missile, and Akash, once development is complete, will be contemporary missiles. The third generation anti-tank Nag will dominate as one of the best such missiles. In any aerospace or missile development programme, delays are possible owing to the technical complexity of the work. But this should not deter us. The propaganda of foreign sellers and their associates in India should not dictate India's procurement decisions. My experience in dealing with the network of institutions that has been established is that our country has tremendous potential to develop the best technologies in this field. India could combat the MTCR very effectively, thereby proving to those who wanted us to fail that 'we can do it'.

Once we had developed competence in the design of missile systems I looked beyond the IGMDP. The natural course of action appeared to be the supersonic cruise missile, which is essential in tactical warfare. Many countries have cruise missiles, but they fly at subsonic speed. Our association with one of the Russian institutes, NPO Mashinostroyeniya, developed into a partnership in the joint design and development of supersonic cruise missile system. This partnership is based upon friendship and equal competencies.

I recall my association with Dr H.A. Yefremov, Director General of NPO Mashinostroyeniya, an outstanding scientist of our time, who had developed seven types of cruise missiles and inducted the systems in the Russian Navy. Creating a joint venture between India and Russia in high-technology projects in the prevailing situation in the 1990s became a complex question and a challenge to both Dr Yefremov and me. Whenever I met Dr Yefremov, I got the feeling of meeting a great scientist like Prof. Satish Dhawan or Dr Werner Von Braun, the father of rocketry. Dr Yefremov took me to his technology centres which are not normally shown to any foreigner. He truly treated me as a friend and arranged an Indian lunch in his laboratory. I took him to the Research Centre Imarat, an advanced missile technology centre at Hyderabad. He was genuinely pleased to see the strides we had made. Our scientific minds merged and our friendship blossomed. We christened the joint venture as BrahMos, a combination of the names of two rivers, the Brahmaputra and the Moscow. Sivathanu Pillai, Ramanathan, Venugopalan and Vice-Admiral Bharat Bhushan, along with the Russian specialists, gave shape to the joint venture. Sivathanu Pillai was the natural choice as the Chief Executive Officer and Managing Director of the joint venture, concurrently holding charge in DRDO as Chief Controller R&D for missiles. The dual role, an exceptional decision of the government, was essential to ensure the success of this venture. Venugopalan, an outstanding propulsion scientist from the Defence Research & Development Laboratory (DRDL), became the Project Director. A new kind of joint venture came into existence, one which bridged the scientific community and industry of the two countries in design, development, production and marketing of an advanced technology weapon. It was a source of great joy for me, as it was for the two teams. The first flight of BrahMos on 12 June 2001 from the Interim Test Range, Chandipur, was a milestone signalling the progress of the joint venture. The second flight, on 28 April 2002, confirmed the results of the first and came as a great encouragement to our effort.

Dr Yefremov and I are glad that both India and Russia have realized that this joint venture is the right way to bridge two friendly nations for building high-technology weapon systems that could enter the world market My dream of marketing an advanced weapon system ahead of the so-called developed countries will come true through BrahMos, even though I am away from the scene. The team that I built has performed creditably. I am happy.

I read a book titled *An Unfinished Dream* by the milkman of India, Dr Verghese Kurien. He says in the book, 'It was by chance that I became a dairy man.' But a British expert's criticism, 'The sewer water of London is bacteriologically superior to the milk of Bombay,' served as a challenge to the young Kurien, who has taken dairying from strength to strength over the decades so that today India is a front-ranker in milk production.

On a visit to Anand I had the opportunity to spend a day with him. As I went around the Amul establishment, I saw value addition at work. From milk the cooperative has branched off to making numerous derivatives, including butter, cheese and ice-cream. These initiatives have given it the strength to be a major player in a highly competitive market. When I asked him what, in his view, was one sure way of launching the country on a growth trajectory, his answer was: 'You must build on the resources represented by our young professionals and by our nation's farmers. Without their involvement we cannot succeed. With their involvement we cannot fail.'

While talking about scientists, I recall my meeting with a medical specialist, Prof. Kakarla Subba Rao, at the Indo-American Cancer Institute at Hyderabad. I asked him if cancer was some unmitigated curse. Yes and no, said the seventy-seven-year-old Albert Einstein Professor of Radiology. Yes, because we genetically inherit certain traits which make us vulnerable to cancer. No, because whether we get it or escape it depends largely on our immune response. Research into how the brain can influence immune response has given rise to the new field called Psycho-Neuro-Immunology (PNI). Findings in this field have brought great hope to people dealing with such difficult illnesses as cancer, AIDS, CFIDS (Chronic Fatigue Immune Dysfunction Syndrome) and other immune-system-related diseases. Other fields of research include Psycho-Neuro-Cardiology (PNC), the study of the mind–heart connection, or Psycho-Neuro-Haematology (PNH), the study of how the mind can influence blood-related disorders, such as clotting problems in haemophilia. Such is the power of thought!

These are diseases which normally require intensive treatment. But even here, medicine acknowledges that our minds can play a major role.

Summary

Vision ignites the minds. India needs visionaries of the stature of J.R.D. Tata, Vikram Sarabhai, Satish Dhawan and Dr Verghese Kurien, to name a few, who can involve an entire generation in mission-driven programmes which benefit the country as a whole.

4

LEARNING FROM SAINTS
AND SEERS

> For the society to prosper there are two important
> needs. They are: prosperity through wealth genera-
> tion and cherishing the value system of the people.
> The combination of the two will make the Nation
> truly strong and prosperous.

I always tell the young to dream. This message comes
from the understanding that each one of us has within
ourselves the ability to create the circumstances for
success—to attract, so to say, to ourselves what we
desire. When as a child Einstein first saw a compass he

was fascinated by the way the needle moved whenever he changed direction. Watching the needle became an obsession with him as he tried to understand the invisible force that moved the compass needle. Where was the force located? Who controlled it? Why did it always work? What was it made of? Were there places where it didn't operate? It is of course the magnetic energy of the earth that keeps pulling the compass needle, a tiny magnet, along the north-south axis of the earth's magnetic field. But is that all there is to it?

We can easily see the magnetic field at work, but cannot detect it with our senses, even though it is everywhere on our planet. Logically then, it is in us also.

Similarly, our planet is in a perpetual state of motion as it goes spinning through space. Everything on the planet is a part of this movement, even though it appears to us that we are motionless. I am on the planet and thus part of the energy that moves it. The energy that is the very essence of the planet is in me.

Dyer argues that we can use this universal energy to bring to us the objects of our desire, because what we desire is also in us and vice versa. It becomes a matter of alignment and will that allows us to tap into this force.

With thoughts like these on the points where science and spiritualism converge, I carved out opportunities to visit a few unique places in a year's time. Most of these places were new to me and offered me the chance to learn more about certain things I had always been interested in but could not explore—such as the world of saints and seers. I saw a diverse range of activities being carried out in the spiritual centres I visited. At one, it was the value-based education being provided that impressed me. At another place, an attempt was being made to integrate ancient science with modern and Sanskrit documents were being studied to gauge the progress made in earlier times. I saw how a Sufi saint could become a magnet for people of different faiths. I had an extended discussion on the fusion of science and spirituality with a guru. I saw how a punya atma can go beyond providing religious strength to setting up hospitals and universities, as also a scheme for supply of water. There was one place which seeks to alleviate the distress of patients who are suffering from terminal cancer. Another centre was exploring the link between medical science and meditation.

My journey started on 13 June 2001, when I met Pramukh Swami Maharaj of Swaminarayan Sanstha at Ahmedabad. My discussion with Swamiji on the fusion of science and spirituality, and the role it could play in national development, went on for an hour. I am tempted to reproduce verbatim the questions and answers with Swamiji.

Abdul Kalam (AK): Swamiji, India had the vision, since 1857, to be an independent nation. It took ninety years for us as a nation to get freedom. During this time the whole nation—the young and old, rich and poor, educated and illiterate—was together in this aim. The goal was one, focussed, and well understood—to acquire independence. Swamiji, what is or what can be such a vision now? Since the last fifty years, India has been a developing country. It means economically it is not strong, socially it is not stable, in security aspects it is not self-reliant, and that is why it is called a developing country. Five hundred members of TIFAC

(Technology Information, Forecasting and Assessment Council) have given thought to what should be the next vision for India. How do we transform a developing country into a developed country in the next twenty years? We have identified five important areas to transform India—education and healthcare, agriculture, information and communication, infrastructure and critical technology. Swamiji, our problem is that we may present this before the government, but how do we create people with values to carry out such a big vision? What we need is a cadre of value-based citizens. Otherwise resources will not be deployed effectively, as we are witnessing. For this, we need your suggestion, Swamiji.

Swamiji: Along with these five, you needed a sixth one—faith in God and developing people through spirituality. This is very important. We need to first generate a moral and spiritual atmosphere. There has to be a change in today's climate of crime and corruption. We need people who live by the laws of the scriptures and bear faith in God. For this we need to rekindle belief. This will make things easier. Our problems will be solved and we shall be able to achieve what we dream.

AK: Swamiji, for carrying forward such a big vision of transforming India, should we first create a spiritual tradition—make people more spiritually inclined—and then embark upon our vision, or focus on one of the important areas like education or health? Or should we integrate everything and begin simultaneously?

Swamiji: We must move ahead simultaneously. Work in the five fields that your team has identified for the country's progress should be continued and this should be concurrently incorporated. Our culture teaches us to learn both Para (spiritual) and Apara (worldly) vidya (knowledge). Therefore, together with knowledge of the Apara, one should learn the Para as well. If one learns this then Apara vidya—worldly knowledge— will become founded on dharma and spirituality. One must remember that in God's scheme of things, the whole purpose behind creation is the idea that every person—every soul—attains bliss.

AK: To realize this great dream, three types of people are needed—punya atma (virtuous people), punya neta (virtuous leaders) and punya adhikari (virtuous officers). If the population of all the three were to increase in our society, then India would become the jagadguru (world leader). How can their numbers be increased?

Swamiji: Together with your academic and scientific training, give spiritual training in our schools and colleges. Nowadays, spiritual education has been removed from the syllabi of schools and colleges. That which should be taught from infancy is being neglected and we continue to provide only academic knowledge. But from the beginning, right from birth, people should be taught values, only then will people become virtuous. Knowledge of our scriptures and great sadhus and sages should be included in the syllabus. The social, spiritual and political leaders whom we hold in respect imbibed the correct values from the very beginning. In the past, such values were taught in our gurukul system of education. Whether a prince or a pauper, everyone studied together. Along with academics, lessons such as satyam vada (speak the truth), dharmam chara (tread the path of righteousness), service towards others and faith in God were taught.

AK: Swamiji, good citizens cannot be produced by the laws of the government. Can spiritual institutions do it? Can you ask parents to guide their children to learn the right values up to the age of fifteen? Similarly, in all elementary schools, teachers should also instil these in the students. But if we fail to do this, then the government cannot by itself produce good, honest citizens. Is my understanding correct, Swamiji?

Swamiji: Yes, it's true. It's definitely true. We've been saying from the very beginning that values should be taught by parents at home, teachers at school, and the guru in later life.

AK: Swamiji, when I first launched a rocket it failed, but strengthened by ISRO's support, my team combated the failure to achieve success. This sentiment is also expressed by Tiruvalluvar in the *Thirukkural*—when failure occurs, challenge it with cheerful attitude.

Swamiji: When one possesses such noble thoughts, patriotism is but natural. That's why we say, if spiritual knowledge is given from the beginning, love and pride for one's country, society and dharma is a natural result. However, spiritual values should form the foundation of life.

AK: Spiritual strength is important. And along with this, we must have economic strength for strength is respected in the world. A combination of both is necessary. And to achieve both, there is only one answer—sweat! Hard work is a must.

Swamiji: We often say, 'Human effort and God's grace.' Even failure of the first rocket, which you faced, was

71

for your good, it prodded you to make things better. God has ultimately given you success.

AK: For India's development, I wish to establish a trust—Vision 2020—with five like-minded individuals. I seek your blessings for this.

Swamiji: God's blessings are already upon you. I shall pray that your ideas are successfully realized. May India prosper both spiritually and economically. What I wish to say is that the stronger the spiritual wealth, the stronger will become all other forms of wealth. If you increase material wealth alone, man will be lost in luxury and worldly pleasures. Spirituality will guide him back, help him rise above mundane pleasures. In reality, we rarely provide what is really needed. We provide everything else, clothing, food, shelter, but with all this we should also provide spiritual wealth. One should remember that when man gains extra money and power, more than what is necessary, then he invites ruin, restlessness and destruction. He loses control.

It's good that you've come here today. It's given us much joy. The rishis (sages) of the past have also given us science. You, too, are a rishi.

*

In September 2001, I visited the Dargah Sharif of Sufi mystic Khwaja Moinuddin Chishti, better known as Gharib Nawaz, at Ajmer. Here, in AD 1256, at the age of 114, the saint entered his cell to pray in seclusion for six days, at the end of which he passed away. As I went round the dargah, I was struck by the beauty of all that the shrine symbolized. Eight hundred years ago, a saint travelled from Arabia, passing through many lands before reaching Ajmer. Here he brought together different communities who lived peacefully around his shrine.

The teachings and message of Khwaja Gharib Nawaz have been of an exceptional character. His simple teachings penetrated even a stony heart; his affectionate look could silence the fiercest enemy; he brought the message of universal love and peace. Chishti sufis who succeeded him continued the tradition set by him. They were truly the pioneers in national integration.

The teachings of Khwaja Sahib have been recorded in several books. For him, one who possesses the magnanimity of the river, the kindness of the sun and humility of the earth is closest to God. Khwaja Sahib said that the noblest character is possessed by one who is graceful in poverty, content in hunger, cheerful in grief and friendly in hostility. According to this great saint, the surest way to avoid the punishment of hell is to feed the hungry, to redress the aggrieved and to help the distressed. Khwaja Sahib gave a role model of Aarif, one who considers death as his friend, comfort as his enemy and always remembers God. An Aarif fears, respects and possesses shyness.

Why can't we conduct ourselves as Aarifs? I wondered. Before any action, ask yourself this question: 'Is what I am about to say or do going to bring me peace?' As Dyer says, if the answer is yes, proceed wholeheartedly with it and you will be allowing yourself the wisdom of your highest self. If the answer is no, be cautious of your ego that is at work. The ego promotes turmoil because it separates you from everyone, including God. At Khwaja Sahib's shrine I could listen to the voice that only wants you to be at peace with yourself.

Ajmer is located in the picturesque Aravalli range. Besides the Dargah Sharif it has the holy lake of Pushkar. These two holy places symbolize, as it were, the abiding amity between the two major religions of India. Ajmer presents a model of a peaceful society. I performed namaz as a thanksgiving for this amity. The scene reminded me of the similar location of two other religious centres, Nagore Dargah and Velankanni church.

On 2 October 2001 I visited Amritanandamayi's Amrita Institute of Computer Technology near Kollam in Kerala with Prof. N. Balakrishnan of the IISc. and G. Madhavan Nair, Director, VSSC. I addressed about 1,000 young students, teachers, brahmacharis and swamis. The topic I selected was 'Multi Dimensions of Knowledge Products.' I found in the students a high level of receptivity to new ideas. In their questions, they showed interest not only in technological development but also in adhering to an honest way of life. After the interaction with the students I met Amma. It was a remarkable experience.

How can one take oneself closer to God was the message she was giving to the people. I wondered at the extraordinary effort that had gone into setting up an institution which could build hospitals, set up management schools of high calibre, and provide housing schemes for the economically weaker sections of society. My query led to a discussion with Amma and the other sanyasis. Though the institution imparts education in all major disciplines of knowledge and creates engineers, medical doctors, management graduates and science research scholars, they are still circumscribed by their individual specialization. Amma suddenly said, 'Something is missing. How to connect?'

What she was referring to was bringing together these capabilities for a joint purpose.

I was at Christ College, Rajkot, getting ready for a function there when there was a call from Swami Nikhileswarananda of the Ramakrishna Mission.

Swamiji requested me to visit his ashram and I had to agree. After the function at Christ College, I rushed to the ashram. It was the time for the evening bhajan and so touched was I by the singers' serene invocation that I sat down with them for nearly fifteen minutes, lost in meditation. Here too I felt the same vibrations as I did while meditating at Swami Vivekananda Hall, Porbandar, the birthplace of Mahatma Gandhi.

On 6 October 2001, the Sankaracharyas of Kanchi organized a very important gathering of farmers from hundreds of villages to launch integrated development through the concept of knowledge-empowered rural development. I was invited to participate. Panchayat heads belonging to various political parties converged at Kanchi to discuss development under a project designed to Provide Urban facilities in Rural Areas (PURA). I was struck by the fact that spiritual leaders were helping focus programmes for development.

When the meeting ended both Acharyas called me for a private meeting. Swami Jayendra Saraswathigal inquired about the crashlanding of the helicopter and blessed me. Swami Vijayendra Saraswathigal conveyed to me that the maulvi of a very famous 300-year-old mosque was waiting in the mutt to take me to the mosque. Swamiji suggested that I visit the mosque.

His message brought to my mind an incident in Paramacharya's time, a decade ago, as told by the former President, R. Venkataraman. Mr Venkataraman showed me the mosque very close to the Kanchi mutt. A few years ago, the mosque jamayath (authorities) and the district authorities decided to relocate the mosque to some other suitable place as its present location was inconvenient both for the mutt and mosque. As a large number of people visit the historic mosque and there are huge gatherings at the mutt too, the traffic was becoming difficult to manage. The mutt would rebuild the mosque in its new location. Somehow this message reached the Paramacharya. He vehemently opposed the whole idea. He said, 'In fact, when at 4.30 a.m. the call for namaz comes from the mosque, it acts as a wake-up call for my divine duties.' And also for many other reasons he was opposed to the relocation of the mosque. He made this clear to both the district authorities and the mutt. The Paramacharya went into mouna vridham—deep silence. Finally, shifting of the mosque was stopped.

I later went to the mosque and met the maulvi and kazi and offered namaz there. About fifty students were learning the Holy Quran. I sat with them and asked them to recite the Alhamthu, the sura that embodies the Quran. In Kanchi, I was privileged to see vedic recitation and recitations from the Quran proceeding side by side. Therein lies the greatness and essence of India. Can Kanchi's integrated approach towards learning become a beacon for us and later for the world?

During the discussion in the Sankara College of Engineering among Sanskrit professors, students and teachers, presided over by the Sankaracharyas, it became clear that ancient Sanskrit literature is a storehouse of scientific principles and methodology, even to the extent of there being texts about how to build a viman (aeroplane). Subjects like physics, chemistry, medicine and ayurveda are, of course, well documented. There was a consensus that the work of our ancient scholars and scientists should be thoroughly examined and where possible integrated with modern science.

An invitation came from the Sri Sathya Sai Institute of Higher Learning at Whitefield for Prof. Rama Rao and me. The day began with a morning prayer at 7.00 followed by a discourse rendered in poetic form. Its subject was how to remove hatred from our hearts— by sacrificing the ego and substituting love in its place. When Sai Baba moved amidst the devotees, the effect of his healing presence on people's pain, difficulties and problems was immediately apparent.

In January 2002, I attended a conference on Medical Technology and Healthcare at Whitefield. All through the conference, which began at 9.30 in the morning and ended at 8 in the evening, Sri Sathya Sai Baba was present. He blessed every presentation and when I finished my five-minute presentation on how technology would transform human life—an example being the cardiac stent that we had made—he got up and blessed me, to the cheers of participants.

I was impressed to see his interest in the conference, as I had been impressed by the speciality hospital at Whitefield that I had visited earlier. He had been told that Chennai was facing a water problem. So, when he announced that he would ensure water flowed to the city, it was more heartening still.

On 3 February 2002, I had an extraordinary spiritual experience when I visited the Brahma Kumari Spiritual Academy at Mount Abu. The deity of the Brahma Kumaris, Shiva Baba, descended on one of the disciples, Dhadhi Gurzar. Before our eyes, her personality changed. Her face became radiant, her voice became deeper as she talked about the four treasures: Knowledge, Yoga, Virtue and Service. We—I, Sivathanu Pillai, and Selvamurthy—were lucky to be called by her to the dais and blessed. As she blessed us she said, 'Bharat will become the most beautiful land on earth.'

My interaction with the Coronary Artery Disease (CAD) patients, popularly known as 'Dilwalas', at the Global Hospital and Research Centre of the Brahma Kumari Academy headed by Dr Pratap Midha, clearly illustrated that the mind-body interaction, a subject I touched upon at the end of the previous chapter, is vital for health which is defined as physical, mental and spiritual well-being. My friend Dr W. Selvamurthy postulated through years of clinical work that yoga and meditation significantly alleviate pain. The experiments, which I had the opportunity of initiating through the Defence Institute of Physiology & Allied Sciences (DIPAS) when I was Scientific Adviser to Defence Minister, include a new approach towards healing through mind–body synchrony. Dr Pratap Midha and Dr Selvamurthy joined together and formulated a unique treatment for cardiac patients. When I reviewed this project, two years back, about sixty patients reported an improved sense of well-being. Now, it has yielded excellent results with 400 patients reporting progress. The treatment included lifestyle intervention with Raja Yoga meditation for stress management, low-fat high-fibre diet for reducing risk of hyper lipidemia and regular aerobic exercise or walking to improve the cardio-vascular and metabolic efficiency. I hope that medical treatment will begin to lay greater emphasis on healing not only the body but also the mind.

During my previous visit to the Brahma Kumari Spiritual Academy at Mount Abu, Sister Usha had given me the task of interacting in a group discussion with thirty Brahma Kumaris who had recently joined. It was a pleasure to look at their bright faces bubbling with enthusiasm. In a post-dinner session when I asked them in turn about their mission in life, the reply was unanimous: to serve the people through spiritual endeavour. Dr Selvamurthy and I were moved to recite a Tamil poem composed 1,000 years ago by Awaiyar which in translation reads thus:

'It is rare to be born as a human being
It is still more rare to be born without any
    deformity
Even if you are born without any deformity
It is rare to acquire knowledge and education
Even if one could acquire knowledge and
    education
It is still rare to do offerings and tapas
But for one who does offerings and tapas
The doors of heaven open to greet him.'

I then narrated to the Brahma Kumaris how the Bishop at Thumba allowed transfer of the land belonging to the church for setting up a space research station (as given in chapter three of this book). What is the conclusion to be drawn from this story? I asked them. The Brahma Kumaris responded by saying that our civilization is rich, which leads to forward thinking, harmony and better understanding. With such a great nation and people, why are there communal clashes? I think that when a nation doesn't have a vision, small minds take over its affairs.

The unification of science and spirituality will be essential to take the benefit of science and technology to mankind. In 1911, Sri Aurobindo wrote in the *Song of Humanity:* 'A time will come when the Indian mind will shake off the darkness that has fallen upon it, cease to think or hold opinions at second and third hand and reassert its right to judge and enquire with perfect freedom into the meaning of its own culture and tradition.'

That is the future we need to work towards as we shake off the shackles of poverty.

There was one message common to all the places I visited—there is a higher self within you that transcends the limitations of the physical world. I felt the presence of this higher self in my father.

I have learned over the years to maintain my equanimity regardless of circumstances. I have faced failures and disappointments without feeling defeated. I wish to live the rest of my life at peace with myself and others. I have no wish to engage in quarrels with others.

This is the challenge before the individual as he tries to transcend his limitations.

At this point, I recall a sura from the Holy Quran.

'O Prophet, you proclaim to the people
Who do not accept your preaching,
What you worship, I do not worship,
And what I worship, you do not worship;
The result of your actions belongs to you,
The result of my actions belongs to me.'

What we are, what we believe in, is ours alone. Once we have trust in the wisdom that created us, we can develop a faith that sustains us through our lives.

Indians are well versed with the concept of higher self, or perhaps highest self is the preferable term. For generations our ancestors lived their lives by this concept. But for many today, rooted perhaps too deeply in the material world, this idea sounds lofty and spiritual. For me it has been a cornerstone of the way I live.

On one occasion, as I was leaving for Bangalore, I spoke to a friend of mine and told him that I would be talking to young people and whether he had any suggestions. He did not offer any suggestions as such, but offered me these nuggets of wisdom.

'When you speak, speak the truth; perform when you promise; discharge your trust . . . withhold your hands from striking, and from taking that which is unlawful and bad . . .

'What actions are most excellent? To gladden the heart of a human being, to feed the hungry, to help the afflicted, to lighten the sorrow of the sorrowful and to remove the wrongs of the injured . . .

'All God's creatures are His family; and he is the most beloved of God who tries to do most good to God's creatures.'

These are the sayings of Prophet Mohammad. My friend who told me this is a greatgrandson of a Deekshidar of Tamil Nadu and grandson of a Ganapathigal (vedic scholar). He is none other than Y.S. Rajan.

Such an outlook is possible only in our country. Let us remember the Rig Veda: 'Aano bhadrah kratavo yenthu vishwathaha.' That is, 'Let noble thoughts come to us from every side.'

I recall an event that took place in my family. My grandfather and greatgrandfather were called Ambalakarar—noble leaders—in Rameswaram. This island has the privilege of being known as the place where Lord Rama is said to have launched his campaign against Ravana. The island celebrates this event by organizing his marriage with Sita—his divine counterpart. My greatgrandfather would provide a floating platform for the occasion to carry the decorated vigraha through the holy tank named Ramar Theertham. The tank is very deep. The floating platform with vigraha, bedecked with beautiful gold ornaments, of Lord Rama is taken round a small mandapa at the centre of the tank.

Then and now, all of Rameswaram assembles for the occasion.

One year, my greatgrandfather was witnessing the event when a mishap took place. The vigraha toppled down and sank. Without any hesitation or prompting, he jumped into the tank and recovered the vigraha as the entire town watched. The temple priests instituted muthal mariathai (first honour) for our family. There was a special prayer in the Rameswaram mosque to thank the Almighty for the recovery of the vigraha and to bring God's grace on our family.

I have always considered this incident as a shining example of human brotherhood and harmony, specially significant in today's context. Could not each of us help nurture such a brotherhood wherever we happen to be?

On 15 August 1947, my high school teacher, Rev. Iyyadurai Solomon, took me to hear the midnight freedom speech of Pandit Jawaharlal Nehru. We were all moved to hear him say that we were free. Banner headlines announced the momentous event in next day's newspapers. But alongside the report of Panditji's speech in the Tamil newspaper I read, was another news item, one that has been embedded in my memory. It was about how Mahatma Gandhi was walking barefoot in Noakhali, to help assuage the pain of the riot-affected families there. Normally, as Father of the Nation, Mahatma Gandhi should have been on the ramparts of Red Fort, the first one to unfurl the national flag. Instead, he was at Noakhali. Such was the Mahatma's greatness, and what an everlasting impact it left on the mind of a schoolboy!

Having sensed the pulse of the young, and armed with the wisdom of the elders, I thought deeply about my own experiences with technology projects where people worked on problems that were new and demanded efforts that were unprecedented. What really makes one succeed in the face of difficult tasks? We have talked about the importance of having a dream and of commitment, of hard work and having the spiritual strength to persevere through difficulties and failures. Is there anything missing in the cycle of creation?

Summary

Our spiritual wisdom has been our strength. We survived as a nation the onslaughts of invaders and the numbing effects of colonialism. We have also learnt to adjust to the rifts and divisions in our own society. But in the process of all the adjustment, we also lowered our aims and expectations. We must regain our broad outlook and draw upon our heritage and wisdom to enrich our lives. The fact that we advance technologically does not preclude spiritual development. We need to home-grow our own model of development based on our inherent strengths.

5

PATRIOTISM BEYOND POLITICS AND RELIGION

> I do not care for liberation, I would rather go to a hundred thousand hells, 'doing good to others (silently) like the spring', this is my religion.
>
> —Swami Vivekananda

Walking has been an essential part of my life. Wherever I go I make it a point to walk five kilometres in the morning. I am particularly attached to seeing the beauty of the sunrise, the light that precedes its arrival and my ears are tuned to the songs that birds sing to welcome the dawning of a new day on this planet. Each time I experience these phenomena—the cool breeze, the singing of the birds and the arrival of the sun—I am filled with awe at how nature brings together all the elements that go into making this moment possible and feel thankful to God.

I have been fortunate in that my work has taken me to very many beautiful places that opened up my mind to the cosmic reality. One such was Chandipur in Orissa.

From Kolkata, the distance to Balasore is around 234 km and Chandipur is 16 km from the town. The name means the abode of the Goddess Chandi or Durga. The beach here is surely among the finest in India. At low tide the water recedes three kilometres as the tides follow their rhythmic cycle.

The lonely beach, the whispering of tamarisk trees and the cool breeze create a feeling of extraordinary calm. I used to walk on the beach to the mouth of the river Suwarnarekha. The river's vast spread and the bewitching, ceaseless ripples of its water were hypnotic in their effect. It was a feeling as close to bliss as I have ever felt.

We started test-firing our missiles from the Sriharikota Range of ISRO but needed our own missile test range. The Interim Test Range (ITR) was established in 1989 as a dedicated range for launching missiles, rockets and flight test vehicles. A number of missiles of different class including the multi-role Trishul, multi-target capable Akash, the anti-tank Nag missile, the surface-to-surface missile Prithvi, and the long-range technology demonstrator Agni have been test-fired from the ITR. BrahMos, the Indo-Russian joint venture set up to develop supersonic cruise missiles, has also been tested at this range. The ITR has also supported a number of other missions such as testing of the multi-barrel rocket launcher Pinaka and the pilotless aircraft Lakshya.

The ITR has also been made capable for testing airborne weapons and systems with the help of sophisticated instrumentation. Thrust areas include tracking long-range missiles, air defence missile systems, weapons systems delivered by the Light Combat Aircraft (LCA), multi-target weapon systems and high-acceleration manoeuvrable missiles.

The ITR extends 17 km along the seacoast where a number of tracking instruments have been deployed along the flight path of the test vehicles. Some of the significant test facilities at the ITR are a mobile and fixed electro-optical tracking system, mobile S-band tracking radar, fixed C-band tracking radar, fixed and mobile telemetry system, range computer, photo processing system, meteorological system and range safety systems. An expert system has been developed for aiding safety decisions during launch. The ITR is slowly but surely growing into a world-class range.

It was a hot and humid midnight sometime in July 1995. We were going through the results of the fourth consecutive successful flight of Prithvi. People's faces were lit up with success. There was a mood of celebration. More than thirty of us, representing 1,200 hard-working team members, were pondering over the question—what next? Lt. Gen. Ramesh Khosla, Director General Artillery, suggested that the Army needed a flight test on a land range with the accuracy of impact at the final destination within 150 meters. This is called Circular Error Probability (CEP) in technical terms.

We opened a geographical map of India. There were five tiny dots at a distance of 70 to 80 km from ITR. These are the Wheeler Islands. We could not go to the Rajasthan desert for obvious reasons. The Andaman and Nicobar Islands are far away. At 2.00 a.m. we decided that Wheeler Islands were the right choice for the missile impact test. Now the search for a suitable island started. A helicopter was used to survey the area. Someone proposed asking the fishermen to guide us to the islands.

My two colleagues, Saraswat and Salwan, drove to a place called Dhamra. From Dhamra, they hired a boat for the day for Rs. 250. By the time they reached the island it was almost dark. Salwan had carried fruits for eating during the journey but these eventually became their dinner. There was no option but to stay on the island. It was a beautiful night but my friends, neither familiar with the sea nor used to being marooned on a deserted island, spent it rather fearfully—though they won't confess it and claim instead that they enjoyed it. Early the next morning, they began their survey of the island, which is about 3 km long and 800 metres wide. To their surprise, they saw on the eastern side of the island a Bangladesh flag flying atop a tree with huts nearby. The island was probably frequented by fishermen from the neighbouring country. My friends quickly removed the flag.

Things moved fast thereafter. The district authorities, including forest and environment officers, visited the island. Soon after, I got the Defence Minister's clearance to acquire the islands. The formalities were gone through with the Orissa government and the forest department to transfer the land. I personally met the concerned senior officials to make the file move to the desk of the Chief Minister. I also wrote a detailed letter to the Chief Minister explaining why we needed the islands for DRDO work, specially for use as a range for experimental purposes.

We had already done preparatory work before moving the application. There were typical questions about fishing activity in the vicinity, the disturbance that might be caused to turtle migration and above all the cost of the islands. Within ten days we got an appointment from the Chief Minister. I had heard a lot about Chief Minister Biju Patnaik, particularly about his days as a pilot and his friendship with President Sukarno. When I entered the Chief Minister's chambers with Maj. Gen. K.N. Singh and Salwan, he welcomed us warmly. To me he exclaimed, 'Oh my friend Kalam, I have followed your work from the time of Dr Sarabhai to now. Whatever you ask, I will give.' In my presence he signed the Orissa government's decision to give to DRDO all the four islands and said, 'Kalam, I have given the approval you asked for, I know you will use it well. Your mission—the missile programme—is very important to the country. Anything needed from Orissa will be yours.' Then, suddenly, he held me and gave me a very affectionate hug. He said in a demanding tone, 'Kalam, you have to give me a promise and assurance to the nation. The day India makes its own ICBM I shall be stronger as an Indian.' There was silence. I had to respond immediately. Biju Patnaik was a man with a tremendous personality and deeply impressive as a leader too, one whose love for the nation transcended politics. I looked straight into his eyes and said, 'Sir, we will work for your mission. I will discuss your thought in Delhi.'

Some forty years ago, the daredevil Biju Patnaik piloted his Kalinga Airways plane into Jakarta to find Indonesian President Sukarno in the first flush of fatherhood. Sukarno's wife had delivered a baby, and the family was searching for a name for the newborn girl when Bijuda called on them.

Sukarno explained the problem on hand to the visitor from India. Biju Patnaik cast his mind back to the clouds that had greeted the baby's arrival and suggested the Sanskrit equivalent for them. Sukarno's daughter was promptly christened Megawati and thus the daughter of the leader of the world's largest Muslim nation got a Hindu name. For great men, religion is a way of making friends; small people make religion a fighting tool.

Many years later, after several political upheavals, Megawati Sukarnoputri would become first the Vice President and then the President of Indonesia.

Lament, my friend, at the passing away of a generation of politicians with a voice, vision and reach that went far beyond our borders. Lament at our State-sponsored, abnormal and paranoid fixation with a particular country that has blinded us to the rest of the world, including the Third World, which we used to head not so long ago. And weep softly at what we have reduced ourselves to in the comity of nations. For a large country with a billion people, a country with a thriving industry and a large pool of scientific talent, a country, moreover, that is a nuclear power, India does not count for as much as it should. In terms of our influence in world affairs, probably no other country is so far below its potential as we are.

After Pokhran II, the West speaks about India and Pakistan in the same breath. Is it not in our national interest to demonstrate to the world that we can think of a world beyond Pakistan, that we are a qualitatively better, more mature and secular country with a greater commitment to the values of democracy and freedom?

During March 2002, I was teaching about 200 final year students of engineering at Anna University and I gave a series of ten lectures on 'Technology and Its Dimensions'. On the final day of the interaction, there was a discussion on Dual Use Technologies. One of the students raised a question.

'Sir, I have recently come across Dr Amartya Sen's statement that the nuclear weapon test conducted in May 1998 by India was ill conceived. Dr Amartya Sen is a great economist and a Nobel laureate who is much respected for his ideas on development. A comment from such a personality cannot be ignored. What is your view on his comments?'

'I acknowledge the greatness of Dr Amartya Sen in the field of economic development and admire his suggestions, such as that thrust should be given to primary education,' I said. 'At the same time, it seemed to me that Dr Sen looked at India from a Western perspective. In his view, India should have a friendly relationship with all countries to enhance its economic prosperity. I agree, but we must also bear in mind India's experience in the past. Pandit Nehru spoke in the United Nations against nuclear proliferation and advocated zero nuclear weapons in all the countries. We know the result. One should note that there are more than 10,000 nuclear warheads on

American soil, another 10,000 nuclear warheads are on Russian soil and there are a number of them in the UK, China, France, Pakistan and some other countries. The START II and the recent agreements between the USA and Russia only talk about reducing the number of nuclear warheads to 2,000 each and even these agreements are limping. Nobody takes the reduction of warheads in serious terms. There should be a movement by those who are against the May 1998 test in America and Russia or other Western countries to achieve zero nuclear weapons status. It is essential to remember that two of our neighbouring countries are armed with nuclear weapons and missiles. Can India be a silent spectator?'

India has been invaded in the last 3,000 years by a succession of conquerors, including the British, French, Dutch and Portuguese, either to enlarge their territory or to spread a religion or to steal the wealth of our country. Why is it India never invaded other countries (with a few exceptions in the Tamil kingdoms)? Is it because our kings were not brave enough? The truth is Indians were tolerant and never understood the true implications of being ruled by others for generations. But after the long independence struggle when we got our freedom and the country got united and has physical boundaries, is it possible to remain with economic prosperity as the only goal? The only way to show the strength of the country is the might to defend it. Strength respects strength and not weakness. Strength means military might and economic prosperity. The decisions and policies of the United Nations Security Council are dictated by the countries who possess nuclear weapons. How is it we did not get a seat in the Security Council so far but now other nations are recommending that India be made a member?

In this regard, there is another incident I would like to narrate. My friend, Admiral L. Ramdas, who retired as the naval chief, told me that he and a group of people would hold a demonstration before Parliament protesting against the nuclear test carried out in May 1998. I replied to my friend that he and his group should first demonstrate in front of the White House and the Kremlin against the large quantity of nuclear warheads and ICBMs there.

I call to my people to rise to greatness. It is a call to all Indians to rise to their highest capabilities. What are the forces which lead to the rise or fall of nations? And what are the factors which go to make a nation strong? Three factors are invariably found in a strong nation: a collective pride in its achievements, unity and the ability for combined action.

For a people and a nation to rise to the highest, they must have a common memory of great heroes and exploits, of great adventures and triumphs in the past. If the British rose to great heights it is because they had great heroes to admire, men like Lord Nelson, say, or the Duke of Wellington. Japan represents a fine example of national pride. The Japanese are proud of being one people, having one culture, and because of that they could transform a humiliating military defeat into a triumphant economic victory.

All nations which have risen to greatness have been characterized by a sense of mission. The Japanese have it in large measure. So do the Germans. In the course of three decades, Germany was twice all but destroyed. And yet its people's sense of destiny never dimmed. From the ashes of the Second World War, it has emerged a nation economically powerful and politically assertive. If Germany can be a great nation, why can't India?

Unfortunately for India, historic forces have not given a common memory to all communities by taking them back to their roots a millennium down the ages. Not enough effort has been made in the last fifty years to foster that memory.

I had the fortune of learning many of our religions in the country from my childhood, in high school and then onwards for nearly seventy years. One aspect I realize is that the central theme of any religion is spiritual well-being. Indeed it should be understood that the foundation of secularism in India has to be derived from spirituality.

It is because our sense of mission has weakened that we have ceased to be true to our culture and ourselves. If we come to look upon ourselves as a divided people with no pride in our past and no faith in the future, what else can we look forward to except frustration, disappointment and despair?

In India, the core culture goes beyond time. It precedes the arrival of Islam; it precedes the arrival of Christianity. The early Christians, like the Syrian Christians of Kerala, have retained their Indianness with admirable determination. Are they less Christian because their married women wear the mangalsutra or their menfolk wear the dhoti in the Kerala style? Kerala's Chief Minister, A.K. Antony, is not a heretic because he and his people are part of Kerala's culture. Being a Christian does not make him an alien. On the contrary, it gives an added dimension to his Indianness. A.R. Rahman may be a Muslim but his voice echoes in the soul of all Indians, of whatever faith, when he sings *Vande Mataram*.

The greatest danger to our sense of unity and our sense of purpose comes from those ideologists who seek to divide the people. The Indian Constitution bestows on all the citizens total equality under its protective umbrella. What is now cause for concern is the trend towards putting religious form over religious sentiments. Why can't we develop a cultural—not religious—context for our heritage that serves to make

Indians of us all? The time has come for us to stop differentiating. What we need today is a vision for the nation which can bring unity.

It is when we accept India in all its splendid glory that, with a shared past as a base, we can look forward to a shared future of peace and prosperity, of creation and abundance. Our past is there with us forever. It has to be nurtured in good faith, not destroyed in exercises of political one-upmanship.

The developed India will not be a nation of cities. It will be a network of prosperous villages empowered by telemedicine, tele-education and e-commerce. The new India will emerge out of the combination of biotechnology, biosciences and agriculture sciences and industrial development. The political leaders would be working with the zeal born of the knowledge that the nation is bigger than individual interests and political parties. This attitude will lead to minimizing the rural-urban divide as progress takes place in the countryside and urbanites move to rural areas to absorb the best of what nature can give in the form of products and wealth.

The most important and urgent task before our leadership is to get all the forces for constructive change together and deploy them in a mission mode. India is a country of one billion people with numerous religions and communities. It offers a wide spectrum of ideologies, besides its geographic diversity. This is our greatest strength. However, fragmented thinking, compartmentalized planning and isolated efforts are not yielding results. The people have to come together to create a harmonious India.

The second vision of the nation will bring about a renaissance to the nation. The task of casting a strong India is in the hands of a visionary political leadership.

Summary

There are success stories among failures. There is hope among chaos, promise among problems. We are one billion people with multiple faiths and ideologies. In the absence of a national vision cracks at the seam keep surfacing and make us vulnerable. There is a need to reinforce this seam and amalgamate us into one national forum.

6

THE KNOWLEDGE SOCIETY

Wisdom is a weapon to ward off destruction; It is an
inner fortress which enemies cannot destroy.
                              —Thirukkural 421 (200 BC)

Ancient India was an advanced knowledge society.
Invasions and colonial rule destroyed its institutions
and robbed it of its core competence. Its people
have been systematically degraded to lower levels
of existence. By the time the British left, our youth
had lowered their aims and were satisfied earning
an ordinary livelihood. India is essentially a land of

knowledge and it must rediscover itself in this aspect. Once this rediscovery is done, it will not require much struggle to achieve the quality of life, strength and sovereignty of a developed nation.

Knowledge has many forms and it is available at many places. It is acquired through education, information, intelligence and experience. It is available in academic institutions, with teachers, in libraries, in research papers, seminar proceedings and in various organizations and workplaces with workers, managers, in drawings, in process sheets and on the shop floors. Knowledge, though closely linked to education, comes equally from learning skills such as those possessed by our artists, craftsmen, hakims, vaidyas, philosophers and saints, as also our housewives. Knowledge plays a very important role in their performance and output too. Our heritage and history, the rituals, epics and traditions that form part of our consciousness are also vast resources of knowledge as are our libraries and universities. There is an abundance of unorthodox, earthy wisdom in our villages. There are hidden treasures of knowledge in our environment, in the oceans, bioreserves and deserts, in the plant and animal life. Every state in our country has a unique core competence for a knowledge society.

Knowledge has always been the prime mover of prosperity and power. The acquisition of knowledge has therefore been the thrust area throughout the world. Additionally, in India, there has been a culture of sharing it, not only through the tradition of guru–shishya but also by its spread to neighbouring countries through travellers who came to Nalanda and other universities drawn by their reputation as centres of learning. India is endowed with natural and competitive advantages as also certain distinctive competencies. But these are scattered in isolated pockets and the awareness of these is inadequate. During the last century the world has changed from being an agricultural society, in which manual labour was the critical factor, to an industrial society where the management of technology, capital and labour provide the competitive advantage. In the twenty-first century, a new society is emerging where knowledge is the primary production resource instead of capital and labour. Efficient utilization of this existing knowledge base can create wealth for us in the form of better health, education and other indicators of progress. The ability to create and maintain the knowledge infrastructure, to enhance skills and increase productivity through the exploitation of advances in various fields will be the key factors in deciding the prosperity of this society. Whether a nation qualifies as a knowledge society is judged by how effectively it deals with knowledge creation and knowledge deployment.

The knowledge society has two very important components driven by societal transformation and wealth generation. The societal transformation is in respect of education, healthcare, agriculture and governance. These will lead to employment generation, high productivity and rural prosperity.

The task of wealth generation for the nation has to be woven around national competencies. The TIFAC task team has identified core areas that will spearhead our march towards becoming a knowledge society. The areas are: information technology, biotechnology, space technology, weather forecasting, disaster management, telemedicine and tele-education, technologies utilizing traditional knowledge, service sector and infotainment which is the emerging area resulting from convergence of information and entertainment. These core technologies, fortunately, can be interwoven by IT, a sector that took off only due to the enterprising spirit of the young.

Thus there are multiple technologies and appropriate management structures that have to work together to generate a knowledge society. With India carving a niche for itself in information technology, the country is uniquely placed to fully capitalize on the opportunity to quickly transform itself into a knowledge society. The methodology of wealth generation in these core areas and to be able to meet an export target set at $50 billion by the year 2008, especially through the IT sector, is a subject that is currently under discussion. Also being discussed is how best to simultaneously develop the capability to generate information technology products worth $30 billion domestically to pump in for societal transformation. I am glad that the

Planning Commission has taken a lead in generating a roadmap for transforming India into a knowledge society. I had the opportunity to be the Chairman of the Steering Committee set up for this task.

Evolving suitable policy and administrative procedures, changes in regulatory methods, identification of partners and, most important, creation of young and dynamic leaders are the components that have to be put in place. In order to generate wealth, which is the second component for establishing a knowledge society, it is essential that simultaneously a citizen-centric approach to shaping of business policy, user-driven technology generation and intensified industry-lab-academia linkages have also to be established.

Becoming a knowledge superpower by the year 2010 is a very important mission for the nation. While a knowledge society has a two-dimensional objective of societal transformation and wealth generation, a third dimension emerges if India is to transform itself into a knowledge superpower. This is knowledge protection and it entails a tremendous responsibility. It is very important that our communication network and information generators are protected from electronic attacks through surveillance and monitoring. There should be a focussed approach to intellectual property rights and related issues, and our ancient knowledge and culture too are part of our resource base and need to be protected as such.

In 1960, the agriculture sector employed in part or in full 74 per cent of the population. This came down to 62 per cent in 1992 and is expected to further fall to 50 per cent by 2010, though the demand of agricultural products will double by then. Higher productivity and better post-harvest management will have to compensate for the manpower reduction in the farming and agricultural products sector.

There was a function in Chennai organized by the Manipal Academy of Higher Education who felicitated me along with the father of the Green Revolution, C. Subramaniam, and eminent lawyer N.A. Palkhivala. After the function, I shared with the ninety-year-old Subramaniam his vision of a second green revolution.

He told me about his dream of setting up a national agro foundation that would develop hybrid seeds. His foundation would adopt small and marginal farmers and provide them with laboratory facilities for soil testing and access to information on the weather and markets, so that they could earn more through enhanced yields and better prices for what they produced. He aimed at bringing a million farmers under the scheme. Visionaries don't age!

On another occasion, I was talking to the students of Dr Mahalingam College of Engineering and Technology at Pollachi, near Coimbatore. Dr N. Mahalingam, a great industrialist and academician, was sitting with me. He was telling me how the country can generate wealth through agro, chemical and textile industries. Amazed by his achievements in establishing industries and educational institutions, I asked him, 'Sir, what is your next mission?' As I said this, I realized I was asking this question of a person who was about eighty years old!

Dr Mahalingam replied, 'I have analysed the Tamil scripts used in the last Sangam, which was 2,500 years ago. Now I would like to do research on the Tamil scripts used in the first Sangam which existed 5,000 years ago!' It was another reminder to me that visionaries don't age.

In the case of industry, in 1960, 11 per cent of the population was engaged in small-scale and large-scale industries. The trend continued with 11 per cent even in 1992. However, it has to increase to 25 per cent in 2010, bearing in mind the envisaged GDP growth and increased competition as trade restrictions are lifted under the WTO. The pattern of employment will take a new shape. Employment in the service or knowledge industry has increased from 15 per cent in 1960 to 27 per cent in 1992. And it will further increase to 50 per cent in view of infrastructure maintenance areas and IT sector and entertainment demands. This big change will demand more trained personnel. Our leaders in commerce and industry have to prepare themselves for the transformation.

The fact that there is net migration from the villages to cities shows the disparities in living standards between the two. Ideally, both rural and urban areas should be equally attractive with no net migration either way. Near zero net rural–urban migration is a mark of development. How can we achieve that happy balance? Rural development is the only solution. This means providing rural areas with the amenities that are currently available only in cities. This would generate employment on the same scale, and at the same level, as in the cities in the rural areas too. The other challenge would be to provide these benefits at a small fraction of the financial, social, cultural and ecological costs the cities have to bear.

It is the expectation that this combination of generating employment bearing in mind environmental factors will make rural areas as attractive as cities are, if not even more attractive. Then, rural development may be expected to prevent, if not actually reverse, rural–urban migration. Hence, PURA aims at integrated physical, electronic knowledge and economic connectivity.

Experience in India has demonstrated that the true handicap suffered by rural areas is poor connectivity and little else. Linking together a loop of villages by a ring road and high-quality transport may rectify that lacuna. Villages thus linked would also provide a large enough market to support a variety of services, which they would not be able to do individually. The ring road and the transport service together can convert the linked villages immediately into a virtual town with a market of tens of thousands of people. Such an area, which would also possess state-of-the-art telecommunication connectivity, will have a high probability of attaining rapid growth by setting up a virtuous cycle—more connected people attracting more investment, and more investment attracting even more people and so on. Basically, this involves selecting a ring of villages; connecting the villages on the ring by establishing a high-quality transport and telecommunication system; encouraging reputed specialists to locate schools, hospitals and other social services around the ring; marketing this well-serviced space to attract industry and commerce; and Internet connectivity.

The model envisaged a habitat designed to improve the quality of life in rural places and made special suggestions to remove urban congestion. Naturally our most intractable urban problem is that of congestion. Efficient supply of water and effective waste disposal in every locality are the paramount civic needs. There is a minimum size below which a habitat is not viable and not competitive with the existing congested city. At the same time, the existing congested city is not economical compared to a new town once a minimum size of expansion is crossed. As against a conventional city that is, say, rectangular in shape and measuring 10 km by 6 km, the model considers an annular ring-shaped town integrating minimum eight to ten villages of the same 60 square km area, and the same access distance of 1 km to transport arteries. It needs only one transportation route of a distance half that needed for the rectangular-shaped city, so frequency of transportation will be doubled, halving waiting times. It has zero number of junctions and needs only one route as against eight needed for the rectangular plan, so people will no longer need to change from one line to another. That saves transport time. Further, as all traffic is concentrated on one single route, high-efficiency mass transportation systems become economical even for a comparatively small population. This cuts costs substantially and is more convenient for the people.

Rural development is an essential need for transforming India into a knowledge superpower and high bandwidth rural connectivity is the minimum requirement to take education and healthcare to the rural areas. Roadmaps for development of certain areas have been generated and we have to work on their realization.

There was an invitation by Mr Ratan Tata, Chairman of the Tata group of companies, to visit Telco at Pune, particularly to witness the challenge of designing, developing and manufacturing in the country a fully Indian car, the Indica. The prospect of the visit excited me. I thought I would get an answer to some questions that I have been asked on many occasions.

In 1980 when our team in ISRO launched the satellite launch vehicle and put Rohini into low-earth orbit, it was a big event for the nation. On

4 January 2001, when I saw the first prototype fighter aircraft, the Light Combat Aircraft (LCA), designed and developed indigenously by the Aeronautical Development Agency (ADA), taking to the skies, again India was described as one of the few countries to have acquired capabilities in this sophisticated field. This is the result of intensified networking between R&D laboratories, industry, academic institutions, users and the government.

Ratan Tata told me during the visit about his vision of making India a global player in the automobile sector. To implement his vision, he decided to acquire car manufacturing units from many countries rather than set them up here at considerable expense in terms of money and time. He looked towards manufacturing five times the present levels so that they could graduate to being globally competitive. This is a beautiful idea. I would add that Indian industrial complexes should become consortia as a first step and then envision becoming multinational companies.

I and my team are invited by a number of scientific, industrial, academic and management institutions to share our experiences in the pursuit of some of the national tasks I have mentioned. One question that came up during my interaction with students in Mumbai rings in my mind even now.

'Dr Kalam, we are very happy to see that India can build and produce its own SLVs and satellites, its own strategic missiles as also nuclear weapons and power stations. Can you tell me when India will design and produce its own passenger car with an Indian engine?'

When I was going through the design, manufacture of component, sub-assembly, integration and testing plants at Telco and was told that the company is producing about 60,000 cars annually, I was reminded of this question. I was not only witnessing the answer to it but also the technological strength of our nation.

I had another opportunity to see a concept take shape when Wipro invited me to participate in a function to mark the commissioning of a mobile heart care clinic at Bangalore in October 2000. This was a collaborative effort of Wipro-GE, Care Foundation and Klenzaids. My friend Arun Tiwari and I provided the system concept for the project. It was a great experience for me. After the inauguration I visited the Wipro-GE Centre that builds specialized medical equipment using advanced technologies. As soon as I entered a young man approached me and pinned a national flag on my shirt. I shook his hand and asked him, 'Young man, will you stay and work for this country?'

He replied, 'Dr Kalam, I am in the profession of working on medical gadgets that are used for diagnosis. I am committed to a profession in which one tries to remove pain. I am needed here.' I was delighted by his answer. The centre itself struck me as a positive collaboration between two nations in the field of healthcare.

After the programme, Azim Premji, who heads Wipro, accompanied me to the DRDO guest house. On the way, he explained how he was trying to assist elementary schools in Karnataka so that more children could be brought into the classroom. As we were having tea at the guest house, I asked him, 'How has Wipro reached its high stature in the business world?'

Premji gave a remarkable answer. 'Dr Kalam, I can say there are three aspects that come to my mind. One: Sweat for generations and the hard work of teams. Two: In Wipro we work for the customer's delight. Three: A bit of luck. The third point will not be of any consequence if the first two aspects are not achieved. In Wipro, what we have tried to do is wealth generation with social concern.'

A common thread runs through the experience of these institutions. It is that we can deliver high-technology systems in spite of control and denial regimes. The presence of a competitive environment, networking capabilities, wealth generation with social concern and above all ignited minds of the young: these are all very important ingredients for building a knowledge society.

Maharishi Patanjali said in the Yogasutra, 'When you are inspired by some great purpose, some extraordinary project, all your thoughts break their bounds: Your mind transcends limitations, your consciousness expands in every direction, and you find yourself in a new, great, and wonderful world.

Dormant forces, faculties, and talents become alive, and you discover yourself to be a greater person by far than you ever dreamed yourself to be.'

That is something addressed to all of us. It is the people of a nation who make it great. By their effort, the people in turn become important citizens of their great country. Ignited minds are the most powerful resource on earth, and the one billion minds of our nation are indeed a great power waiting to be tapped.

Summary

Ancient India was a knowledge society that contributed a great deal to civilization. We need to recover that status and become a knowledge power. We must learn from our mistakes to achieve a better standard of life. A developed India will supplant a spirit of defeat with the spirit of victory.

7

GETTING THE FORCES TOGETHER

Determine that things can and shall be done, and
then we shall find the way.

—Abraham Lincoln

As our experience reveals, progress is rapid wherever
there is an efficient administrative set-up, a high level
of education and minimum political interference in
development activity. To me, development is a security-
centric phenomenon—from poverty to food security,
social security and thereafter national security. In
India 2020, we have identified five areas where India
has a core competence for integrated action.

First among these five is agriculture and food processing, where we have to set a target of 360 million tonnes of food and agricultural production. Agriculture and agro food processing, particularly by way of value addition, would bring prosperity to the rural people and speed up economic growth.

The second area is power. A reliable supply of electricity in all parts of the country is a must.

The third area is education and healthcare. Here we have found that education and healthcare are interrelated. For example, Kerala with high literacy and better healthcare could bring down the rate of population growth and improvement in the quality of life in the state. Similarly, in Tamil Nadu too we have seen a fall in the birth rate that is linked to these factors. Studies in Andhra Pradesh indicate a similar trend. These trends need to be replicated in states like Bihar and Uttar Pradesh, where levels of population growth remain high.

The fourth area is information technology. This is one of our core competencies and holds the potential to rapidly transform backward areas, besides promoting education and generating wealth.

The fifth area is the strategic sector. This area, fortunately, has witnessed growth in areas like nuclear, space and defence technology.

Action in these five areas, properly integrated, would lead to food, economic, social and national security. A strong partnership between the research and development institutions, universities, industry and the community as a whole with the government departments and agencies will be essential to accomplish the vision. The key to success lies in connectivity.

The development of education and healthcare will yield the benefits of smaller families and a more efficient workforce. It is the key to employability and social development. Improvements in the agricultural sector, including that of food processing, would lead to food security, employment opportunities and rapid economic growth. Growth in the information technology sector would assist rapid economic growth as well as play an important part in speeding up development. Electric power provides energy security so crucial for all sectors. The strategic sector has a direct impact on industry, sustaining growth and technological strength. For balanced development, all the five areas are of importance. The combined effect of these five areas would result in GDP growth rising from present 6 per cent to 10 per cent and the lives of 300 to 400 million people who are presently living below the poverty line would be significantly improved.

I worked with TIFAC teams in three areas—agriculture, advanced education and rural connectivity. In doing so, I drew on my earlier experiences in the mission areas of sugar, fly ash and composites. With Prof. S.K Sinha, a renowned agricultural scientist, TIFAC took up a project to enhance agricultural productivity in central Bihar and eastern India. Six villages in one and nine villages in the other region were selected during the kharif season of 1998. The system approach consisted of soil analysis, seed choice, cultivation season, fertilizer selection and training to the farmers. This intensive collaboration of scientists and farmers resulted in substantial increase in wheat yields, which rose from 2.5 tonnes per hectare to nearly

5 tonnes per hectare. When I and Y.S. Rajan visited a few villages where this system approach is used, we found the farmers showing an interest in new issues like equipment for faster harvesting, storage facilities and marketing and banking systems. It was clear that a small team, cutting across various departments, could work wonders even in a difficult region, achieving results in a cost-and time-effective way.

Another experiment under way is REACH (Relevance and Excellence in ACHieving new heights in education institutions). The purpose of this mission is to establish 80 to 100 centres that follow common academic programmes and share the commitment to achieve excellence. In this endeavour, they work together by interchange of faculty and joint research as need be. As part of this, Centres of Relevance and Excellence (CORE) have been established in Patiala, Dibrugarh, Mumbai, Thanjavur and Surat in the areas of agro and industrial biotechnology, advanced computing and information processing, petroleum reservoir engineering, industrial safety, environmental engineering and herbal drugs. Our experience in the

REACH programme is that industries are willing to participate in specialized areas of their interest and they are also willing to invest about 40 per cent of the total expenditure in establishing CORE. In return, they will benefit in terms of skilled manpower and access to the results of research. The willingness of industry to be partners in technology development and education has helped our confidence a great deal. It was also satisfying to see Dr M.S. Vijayaraghavan, Adviser in the office of the Principal Scientific Adviser, blossom into a leader in the integrated learning system. His innovation was to bring the commitment of industry to the learning programme.

Another example relates to the programme for rural connectivity evolved under the leadership of Prof. P.V. Indiresan, who was formerly Director of IIT Madras. As mentioned earlier, the fact that there is net migration from villages to cities indicates that they offer more opportunities, and the only way to equalize the flow is to develop the rural areas and bring life there on par with that in the cities. Once employment opportunities increase there, as do the amenities available, as per the model created by Prof. Indiresan, rural development may be expected to prevent, if not actually reverse, rural–urban migration. Presently, several technologies exist to make this possible, provided we use the connectivity approach in various areas.

For the rural development programme called PURA, we have introduced the concept of dynamic connectivity of four types called PEEK: Physics, Electronics, Economics and Knowledge connectivities. One more important need is IT-driven telemedicine.

In May last year, I visited the CARE Hospital in Hyderabad. The whole place had been geared up for a telemedicine trial and the hall was full of doctors, communication engineers, computer scientists and software experts. Patients were to be tested and advised through telemedicine. The patients would undergo electrocardiography and tests for liver functioning. The novel thing was that the patients were in a distant place, but the diagnosis would be done in Hyderabad.

The doctors and the patients interacted via satellite. The ECG data was exchanged with high-resolution image transfer and clinical information provided in real time. I could see the ultrasound images of liver and heart functioning of the patients coming from a faraway hospital as specialists gave their opinion. It looked like a very promising way to offer healthcare services in places that did not have the medical facilities of a large city. Telemedicine could take advanced medical technology to the rural villages and help link up primary health centres, area hospitals, district hospitals and speciality hospitals in the state capitals. To me it was fascinating to see how it brought together engineering and medical science to treat a patient irrespective of distance, using advances in satellite communication and transmission of data.

It was in 1990, on a recommendation of a friend of mine, that I visited Aravind Eye Hospital at Madurai for an eye check-up and treatment. Upon entering I saw an orderly queue of patients awaiting their turn and joined it. The queue was a long one but it was moving fast and within half an hour I was being examined by Dr G. Natchiar and recommended treatment. That done, I went to deposit the money for admission to the hospital. However, I had trouble paying at the counter as the girl there refused to accept a cheque, and I had no cash. I went to Dr Natchiar again and told her my predicament. She considered briefly and agreed to admit me. I was treated and discharged after a few days. A few days later, I received a letter from Dr Natchiar apologizing for not having recognized me. She came to know only when my security personnel enquired about me at the hospital after my discharge.

I have visited the hospital often after that first visit. Dr G. Venkataswamy, brother of Dr Natchiar, is a good friend, and I make it a point to meet him every time I visit Madurai. Let me tell you a little more about Dr Venkataswamy and his commitment to his work. The Aravind Eye Hospital handled more than 1.3 million outpatient visits in 2001. It conducted 190,000 surgeries and held about 1,500 eye screening camps. No wonder then that Dr Venkataswamy's hard work has achieved recognition from WHO. The hospital provides training to students from leading universities abroad, including Harvard and Johns Hopkins.

Dr Venkataswamy has become a superb surgeon despite what to many in his position would be a crippling handicap: his fingers are twisted and frozen by arthritis that struck him while he was a student in medical school.

One day, as we were talking he narrated this incident to me. An industrialist from Delhi came to Dr Venkataswamy and said, 'I need to build a hospital, and I am very much impressed with your hospital. Will you come and start a hospital in Delhi for me?'

Dr Venkataswamy asked him, 'What is it that you want? You have the money; it is not difficult for you to put up a hospital in Delhi. Why don't you just do it?'

The industrialist said, 'No, I want a hospital with the Aravind culture, people are cordial here. They seem to respect people more than money. There is a certain empathy or compassion that seems to flow from them.'

My own experience at the hospital bore this out. In the Aravind experience I see the path that we need to take—a transformation of life into a powerful instrument of right action.

As with medicine, in the same way, we shall see technology allied to different fields, such as agriculture. But the overall purpose has to be to help the people and meet their needs.

The vision of a developed India can be realized only if we recognize that wealth generation and wealth protection are two sides of the same coin. A nation's wealth represents the sweat and hard work of its people. The famous Tamil poet Andal, who was regarded as one of the thirteen Vaishnavite Alwars, in her famous work *Tiruppavai* invokes the blessings of God to provide in plenty Neengatha Selvam (stable wealth) to the land. This is possible only with an integrated approach towards development. Granted planners look individually at the activities of various ministries and approve their action plans. However, if these proposals were to be looked at not in isolation but in the context of multiple-use planning, the benefits would multiply. Thus a technology, product or a service resulting out of a particular programme of a department/ministry should be mandated to be available to other departments/ministries at the stage of plan approvals. This would provide the needed integration at the planning stage. A similar approach needs to be put in place at other downstream activities. An integrated mission approach would permit interweaving of measures to generate wealth with similar steps for wealth protection. This is the hallmark of a developed country and hence the key to a developed India.

Another aspect of a developed country is global competitiveness of its industry. It is not only catering to the home market but also aiming for a large market outside it. Hence, its contribution to GDP is also very large. This is a prerequisite for India too in its development. Indian industry has to show the same competitiveness and innovation so that we can have our own multinationals.

Universal literacy and access to education for all is another fundamental requirement for a nation to be truly developed. Education would result in the creation of a large base of people who excel in various fields as well, an invaluable resource for any country.

At present, however, there is a high degree of asymmetry in the educational system. While there are many who aspire to higher education, quality institutions to impart this are few. This creates a large mismatch of demand and supply in quality manpower and is starkly evident in emerging sunrise areas such as information technology, biotechnology, environmental engineering and manufacturing technology. The economic liberalization taking place will only intensify such demand in coming years. Moreover higher education has also to be made more relevant to industry and society, an aspect in which it is inadequate at present.

One solution lies in fostering institutions with expertise in selected subjects of relevance to industry and society. Some of the institutions which have excelled this far could provide templates for the new ones. Lastly, the solution should be implemented in a mission mode—only the mission objectives should be paramount and all else subservient to these objectives.

To develop to the desired level, industry also needs to recognize the importance of forward and backward linkages. While linkages with bridging institutions such as think tanks, technical/consultancy services, other firms involved in similar activities as well as customers constitute the forward linkage, partnership with universities, R&D labs and technology-providing institutions would form the backward linkage. Investment in higher education is therefore crucial for forming this backward linkage which would serve as a springboard for Indian industry to make the jump to becoming a global player. We should not hesitate to take a fast decision for establishing twenty more IITs and medical institutions; whether they are promoted by Indian or foreign groups does not matter as long as the bottom line remains excellence.

On 15 October 2000 a website designed for me by friends in the Ponn Group was launched by the Infosys Chairman, N.R. Narayana Murthy, in the presence of Prof. N. Balakrishnan of the IISc. Some of my friends asked me to post a few questions on the website. My questions were three. First: 'India has been a developing country for more than half a century. What would you as young boys and girls like to do to make it a developed India?' The second question was, 'When can I sing a song of India?' and the third, 'Why do we love anything foreign in spite of our capabilities in many fields, whereas other countries celebrate their own successes?' My only stipulation was that the answer should come from youth aged under twenty.

More than a hundred answers and suggestions were received from within the country and abroad. Five of these answers are relevant here.

One young man from Chandigarh responded, 'I will become a teacher (rather, a professor of engineering) since I am good in, as well as enjoy, teaching and I believe that one of the best ways in which to serve one's nation is to be either a professor or a soldier . . .' A girl wrote from Pondichery, 'A single flower makes no garland. I will . . . work for a garland leading to unity of minds, as this is needed for transforming India into a developed country.' A twenty-year-old youth from Goa responded, 'Like an electron ceaselessly moving in its orbit, I will work ceaselessly for my country, now onwards.'

With reference to the second point I had raised, a young man from Atlanta wrote: 'When India becomes capable of imposing sanctions against any country, if they are needed, then I will sing a song of India.' What the young man meant was that economic strength brings prosperity accompanied by national strength. The fifth answer is actually something that 30 per cent of the respondents said: the need for greater transparency in various facets of our life. One crucial fact often overlooked is that India has a population of 700 million people below the age of thirty-five. These are 700 million people with the inclination, the ability and the enthusiasm to take the nation to greatness. It is a very big force for change indeed.

How can one ignite the young minds? How can one attract and involve the young in the task of nation building? Only a united vision launched with renewed vigour will bring the young force into action.

The subject of transparency and values brings to my mind Gandhiji. I happened to meet in Delhi his granddaughter, Sumitra Kulkarni. I asked her, 'Sumitraji, is there a particular incident (in respect of honesty in public life) that you always remember from your grandfather's life?'

She narrated to me this story. 'Every day, as you all would have heard, Mahatma Gandhi held a prayer meeting at a fixed time in the evening. After the prayers there would be a collection of voluntary gifts for the welfare of harijans and others. The devotees of Gandhiji used to collect whatever was given by the people of all sections and this collection was counted by a few members suggested by Gandhiji. The amount so collected would be informed to Gandhiji before dinner. The next day, a man from the bank would come to collect the money for deposit.

'Once the man reported that there was a shortage of few paise in the money handed over to him and the amount informed to Gandhiji the previous night. Gandhiji, on hearing this, was so upset that he went on fast saying that this is a poor man's donation and we have no business to lose any of it.' This episode is a unique example of transparency in public life. Well, in the same country we are witnessing the best and the worst. We should all, particularly the young generation, launch a movement for a transparent India, just as our fathers fought for our freedom. Transparency is a cornerstone of development.

We have spoken about our progress since independence. We are self-sufficient in agriculture, lead the world in milk production, have made enormous strides in industrial development and so on. However, we are still a developing country, one among hundreds.

As such, it is important to understand where we stand in terms of competitiveness. A country's competitiveness is defined as 'the ability of a national economy to achieve sustained high rates of economic growth'. By that yardstick, according to the global competitiveness report prepared by the World Economic Forum, Singapore is first, the USA is second, Hong Kong is third, Taiwan is fourth, Canada is fifth, the UK is eighth, France twenty-third, Germany twenty-fifth and India fifty-ninth.

What decides world competitiveness? It is a combination of the progressiveness of industry, the push for improved technology and the status of governmental deregulation. In terms of overall GDP size, we are twelfth in the world; in terms of per capita GDP we are fifty-seventh. Is this status acceptable to us? Especially to the young? I believe we should work for fourth or fifth position in terms of GDP as well as in respect of competitiveness. The target year should be 2020 and we should aim for a higher position afterwards. We have discussed some of the strategies and tools that can help us acquire the desired status.

To reiterate, a knowledge society can form the foundation for such a vision. I am glad that the Planning Commission has taken a lead in generating a roadmap for us to become such a society.

Where do we start? A number of new states have been created recently and these provide an excellent opportunity to begin. These states are poorly developed in spite of their abundant natural resources. There is widespread poverty though their people toil and sweat. What really prevents us from leaving the beaten track and venturing upon a new path? The question is not who would allow us but rather, who can stop us?

Summary

We need to adapt the implementation of our programmes and policies into a mission mode to succeed. Progress cannot be swift and far-reaching if the path is full of potholes. The abundant national resources, human and material, remain to be fully utilized.

8

BUILDING A NEW STATE

If I were to look over the whole world to find out the country most richly endowed with all the wealth, power and beauty that nature can bestow—in some parts a very paradise on earth—I should point to India.

—F. Max Müller

I began this book with my travel to Jharkhand state in the month of September 2001. That was my fourth visit. The first two visits brought me very close to the core competence that this state possesses. I have been made patron of the Science and Technology Council of this state. My purpose on this visit was to work out a developmental programme in the area of herbs, forest products and other natural resources after meeting with the Chief Minister, Babu Lal Marandi, the Minister for Science and Technology, Samaresh Singh, and concerned officials. When I landed at Ranchi a group of boys and girls greeted me with lots of flowers. I was quite moved by their regard for a simple scientist and their trust in his dreams. I also met the Governor, Prabhat Kumar, who told me about the hard-working nature of the people and the forest wealth of the state.

I recalled my earlier visit to the hill region about 75 km away from Ranchi. Prof. Basu was spearheading a programme oriented towards children's education and health. As I met the people of the hill region, young and old, in the village complex, sitting like them on the ground, one thing was clear to me: my presence here was ordained. The components for development were all there—a fertile area with good rainfall, tall trees and rich vegetation, and people who were willing to work hard. Their faces were lit up with happiness so pure it is rarely seen any more, in the cities at least.

However their bodies looked tired, showing signs of excess work for a bare livelihood.

On this visit, we made some headway in drawing up a viable plan for developing a herbal drugs industry in the state. We discussed in detail with various officials plans for herbal farms and marketing the herbs to drug producers. Our purpose was that the drugs be manufactured within the state itself so as to provide increased income to the state from value addition as also boost industry there. This was a new experiment for the state and also for our mission, but one that, given our experience in mission management, offers tremendous scope for Jharkhand to enter into three areas in a big way—floriculture, herbs and herbal products.

After the meeting we started for Bokaro, the steel city. The weather was cloudy and we wondered if the flight would be cancelled. We reached Ranchi Airport at 2.30 in the afternoon. A Pawan Hans helicopter had been hired by the state government. I asked the pilot whether we could fly in this weather. All smiles, the pilot promised me a beautiful flight and so the helicopter took off, with myself and two other passengers.

I have often flown in a helicopter but did find the weather particularly rough on this occasion. However, the pilot was skilful and I even congratulated him at one point for keeping the flight smooth in spite of the turbulence. It was a marvellous experience as we flew over vast stretches of forest and hills and streams. I was struck by the clean environment. I wondered whether this precious natural wealth could be conserved from mindless destruction for short-term business gains. With such thoughts in my mind, I noticed that we had started descending.

Suddenly I found the two pilots in agitated discussion regarding the falling RPM count. I became alert myself. Looking down, I could see a large number of cars and people everywhere. Then the crash; the helicopter hit the ground with a shattering sound. Broken parts flew around us and I could see fire engines rush towards us.

I simply got out of the helicopter that had hit the ground as a dead weight. Fortunately the engine failed while we were quite close to the ground. Had it failed moments earlier we could have perished under the impact of the free fall. The pilots were in a state of shock and looked at me helplessly. I held their hands and thanked them. I said, sometimes it happens with flying machines and as pilots they have to face it with courage.

I had to address the Chinmaya Vidyalaya students and they would all be waiting, so we rushed to the school leaving behind the crash and the shock. The school's principal, Krishnaswami, received me and the students showered rose petals as I walked to the dais through the auditorium. News of the crash had preceded my arrival. The children sat in pindrop silence.

To ease the tension I told the young gathering, 'Friends, when I was travelling from Ranchi to here, I admired God's great gift to the state. Under the ground and above it, you have minerals in abundance. The rich soil of the Jharkhand plains can give bountiful crops. When I was flying over the lovely forests and the valleys and hills the thought of the wealth they hold in terms of forest and herbal products was very reassuring. On the ground I saw a fully operational steel plant. Now what I see in front of me and what the new state is famous for is its industrious people. So this state has all the wealth needed. It is a land waiting for a transformation to occur. I see in the future, villages that will be provided with urban facilities and are self-contained in respect of education, health and occupation. Today's incident will help define my remaining life's mission. I forgot my inconvenience during the landing after seeing the state's wealth. How can you use this core competence to become a developed state? For that you have to work in the mission mode.'

At the time these children would be entering adult life and taking up careers, they could be part of a national endeavour to becoming a knowledge society. Their contribution to the state itself could be tremendous. That should be their goal: to make Jharkhand great.

One thing that came to mind constantly as I went round the exhibition put up by the children and watched their performances—including a marvellous peacock dance—was how important it was to improve the education system so that it did not stifle these powerhouses of creativity. I felt this is one area I must work upon with the state and the Centre.

I continued with my other engagements after the function at the Chinmaya Vidyalaya. There was a meeting due at the town hall and I went there, brushing aside the concern of the doctors thoughtfully sent by the General Manager of the Bokaro Steel Plant to look after my well-being. At the town hall the subject I had to speak on was 'Jharkhand's Core Competence and Industries'. I kept my speech short, preferring to let a discussion develop.

Meanwhile, the electronic media had done its job! As there was a strong media presence to cover our arrival, news of the crash travelled quickly throughout the country. I started receiving calls on my mobile phone to find out whether I was all right. I did not want to disturb the meeting and gave the mobile phone to Dr Vijayaraghavan, who by then had reached by road from Ranchi. I asked him to call my elder brother in Rameswaram, who is eighty-six years old, and tell him I was fine. The other call I asked him to make was to my personal secretary Sheridon to handle the calls that would come in.

As I was giving my talk Dr Vijayaraghavan passed a note to me. 'Your brother is not convinced that you are OK. If you are OK he has to hear your voice.' An elder brother remains elder all your life! I interrupted my speech to reassure my brother.

To come back to the discussion at the town hall meeting, I was asked a very pertinent question from the audience. 'Dr Kalam,' the questioner said, 'could you please tell me why is raw material exported from many ports specially designed for this purpose?' This was specially relevant to Jharkhand with its huge storehouse of mineral wealth. In answer, I narrated a conversation I had in Goa. I was on a boat crossing the harbour, on my way to the university for a convocation address, and accompanying me was Dr Jose Paul, Chairman of the Mormugao Port Trust. We started discussing iron ore exports to Japan, much of which take place from Panjim. He told me, 30 million tonnes of iron ore is exported annually from the four ports; of this 17 million tonnes is exported from Mormugao alone. The ore is sold at rather a low price—a few dollars a tonne—as, according to the buyers, it is of inferior quality. As such, its sale did not contribute anything much to the economy. The same ore, utilized here, would, of course, generate far more income because of value addition.

'What is value addition and could you give an example?' I was asked in Bokaro and a powerful example came to my mind. When we were working on the satellite launch vehicles in the 1970s, a requirement arose for beryllium diaphragms. These are used in gyros, sensors used to determine the attitude (the position of an aircraft in relation to specified directions) of the rockets or missiles when they are in flight. As these were not available with us, a procurement team was formed to purchase them in the international market. The team was headed by T.N. Seshan, better known now as the former Chief Election Commissioner of India, with Madhavan Nair, Dr S.C. Gupta and I as members. We struck a deal with a company in New York for a hundred beryllium diaphragms.

Three months later, we got a message from the company that since beryllium diaphragms are used to make gyros mounted on intercontinental ballistic missiles, they did not have permission from the State Department to supply them to India. We immediately initiated action to redress the problem in our typical fire-fighting manner. Technology denied was, to us, technology gained.

Meanwhile, it emerged that India has one of the largest deposits of beryllium ore. The ore was exported in those days to Japan, who processed the ore into beryllium rods and sheets and exported them to US companies to transform them into beryllium products such as diaphragms! I received the shock of my life: this was material mined in India and exported to Japan, who processed it and exported it to the US, and the US company refused to give it to India. Where was our sense of initiative? What had happened to our aims? The issue figured prominently in the press and export of beryllium ore was stopped.

The same story is repeated in other areas. The upshot is that India is poor as a nation in spite of its enormous wealth because it does not focus on value addition, be it in mineral or biodiversity products or even grain or fish. In the case of beryllium ore, value addition by at least ten times takes place in refinement itself. Value addition by at least 100 times is achieved during product conversion. And this is what we would be paying Japan or the US, for something that originated from India itself. It is the same with iron ore, and many other exports; only the scale of value addition varies. It is a lesson that must be quickly learnt.

At the same meeting, another interesting question came up. 'Do you think in politics, purity is possible?' It was a little outside my purview but there was one aspect to it, raised earlier, which I would like to mention. This aspect is that an entire generation of people representing excellence in all fields—politics, industry, sciences, the arts—emerged in the years leading to independence. Mahatma Gandhi, C.V. Raman, J.R.D. Tata, Pirojsha B. Godrej, Laxmanrao Kirloskar, Ramakrishna Bajaj, Rabindranath Tagore, Dr S. Radhakrishnan, Madan Mohan Malaviya . . . it is a long list. Suddenly there was excellence in every sphere of society and the circumstance making such flowering possible was the vision that the nation had set for itself.

I believe if the nation forms a second vision today, leaders of a stature to suit our ambition will appear once again, in all walks of life, including politics.

The next day, I travelled to Bokaro Steel Plant, the largest steel plant in India. The General Manager of the plant, Mr Tiwari, accompanied me. The scale of the plant was breathtaking. I saw hundreds of men working in an organized way as the sweat poured off their bodies, while the molten steel flowed from the furnace like a river on fire. The iron ore would be available for years, I was told. Impressive as the plant was I was disappointed to see that there were no industrial estates around it, utilizing the steel produced here to make various products. I was told that setting up of industrial estates came under state purview. It brought back my old regret at our compartmentalized thinking. Why this fragmented governance where one agency is alienated from another? Unless development is directed towards state-based industries, working on huge national missions through centralized planning will not do much for real prosperity.

On the flight back to Delhi, I wondered how Jharkhand could best be helped. What was needed were a few major missions to transform the state and a time-frame. The state and the Centre would need to make an integrated effort. Would it be possible?

Let me go back to my experience in the SLV-3 missile and weapons development programmes. They illustrate what I mean by an integrated approach. To succeed in these efforts, we had to adopt a multi-organizational mission mode. Building a rocket is a long process from the drawing board to development and launch. All through the process, a number of reliability factors matter. The first stage is a robust booster rocket system. Before Rohini was put into orbit, the booster rocket had gone through five static trials in the flight hardware in full scale, and it had also been tried out during two experimental flights. That means a proven, developed booster was available when the time came for launch.

An IRBM was not demanded by anyone when the missile programme was conceived in 1982. However, the availability of the SLV-3 booster led to the building of a technology demonstrator— Agni—as part of the approved programme. Agni was launched successfully in 1989 at a moderate budget of Rs 36 crore! Nobody in the world could have anticipated India acquiring IRBM capability in the short period of six years. It happened only because the Agni mission was organized into a multi-institutional programme.

My assessment based on various space and defence projects done as mission mode programmes is that intensive partnership between various participants— government departments, industry, research institutions—brings faster development at lower cost. The same holds in other projects and schemes. Central and state projects integrated as mission mode operations will bring rapid development at minimum cost.

What is keeping us from taking this concept further? Does it sound risky to abandon the time-tested route of checks and balances and go in for a tightrope walk? Or is it that going into mission mode would demand a responsibility: Either one has to show the result or quit?

In October 2001, I got the opportunity to visit Guru Gobind Singh Indraprastha University in Delhi. The topic I selected for my address to the students was 'Responsible Young Citizens'. I put forth the importance of India becoming a knowledge society. After the talk, one student asked me an important question, 'Could you tell me why Indians, particularly educated Indians, excel when they go to the USA and Europe? They become rich also.'

I said, 'Recently, I read a book—*The Horse that Flew* by Chidanand Rajghatta which is about Indians who have succeeded in the IT field, especially in America. One quality I noticed in all of those who excelled was that they did not work solo. They worked with their colleagues, irrespective of religious or other differences, and they were not afraid to take risks, starting with the risk of going to a foreign land.'

I met B. Chandrasekhar, who has been a big success as an entrepreneur in Silicon Valley, when he contributed to our alma mater, Madras Institute of Technology (whose acronym, MIT, is the same as that of the famous institute at Massachusetts) to start an Internet Technology Centre. One fine morning Chandrasekhar sold his 10-billion-dollar company to start another enterprise. When I asked him how he took such chances to build his enterprise, Chandrasekhar told me he loved taking risks. There was one other aspect to the success of his and other companies. For them survival depended on performance. And the better they performed, the richer they became.

I have an experience to tell in this regard. It was 1955. I was in the second year of my course in Aeronautical Engineering in Madras Institute of Technology. Our Director was Dr N. Srinivasan, an aeronautical engineer himself. I was working on a project surpervised by him on designing a low-level attack aircraft. A seven-member student team was allotted this task. Three of them—Vivekanandan,

Mahabaleshwar Bhat and I—were given the task of system integration. Our team was supposed to provide the design report with all the drawings in three months' time. Because data on the engine, control system and some other sub-system drawings coming from my friends got delayed, I also got delayed by more than two weeks in submitting my drawings.

It was a humid evening in the month of August. I was working on the drawing board. Dr Srinivasan, on his way to the tennis court, peeped into my room and looked at my work. He realized that I was nowhere near completion. He said, 'Kalam, if you do not complete it in three days' time your scholarship will be stopped.'

That was a big jolt for me. The scholarship was my lifeline, as my father could not afford the high cost of education at MIT. I had to make the best use of the time available. Three days was too short a time to complete it. I would have to work continuously. And this is what I decided to do. I slept on a bench in the college for three nights and went out only for food.

Exactly after three days, Dr Srinivasan visited my drawing board. He spent nearly one hour examining what I had done and said, 'This is good. You have performed a few weeks' work in a few days.' Coming from him, it was a great compliment.

I realized then that if something is at stake, the human mind gets ignited and working capacity gets enhanced manifold. Challenges throw up opportunities. Once one selects a task, one should get immersed in it. Either you will succeed or fail: that risk will always be there. This should not deter you. When you fail, you still have the experience gained to draw upon in the future.

Start by risking your own position for a mission. Either I deliver or I go. Prepare yourself for the endeavour. With effort and perseverance you will succeed. There is always a risk involved when we venture into something new. After all, the process of birth itself is a risky affair. But then the infant starts breathing . . . and life follows, with all its hopes and aspirations. Breathe in thoughts of success and you will be a success.

Summary

The way to development is through purposeful activity. The young especially have to be guided properly, so that their lives find a proper direction and their creativity is allowed to flower. To facilitate this, certain educational reforms must be initiated.

With regard to improving the pace of development, Centre-state efforts should be coordinated in a few key areas and efforts across sectors and organizations integrated and taken up in a mission mode. The mindset must change, showing willingness to take pragmatic risks. Success will follow.

9

TO MY COUNTRYMEN

Where the mind is without fear and the head is held
   high
Where knowledge is free
Where the world has not been broken up into
   fragments . . . .
My Father, let my country awake.

                                    —Rabindranath Tagore

All through this book I have spoken about the power
of the imagination. It lies at the heart of the creative
process and is the very substance of life, allied as it is
to the power to attract to us what we most desire. This

power makes all the difference between the winners and the losers. I would like to see in twenty years a literate and poverty-free India. I dream of an India governed by noble leaders. I dream of a system where the work of scientists and technologists is focussed on specific missions driven by goals relevant to the common man. How is this dream to be made real?

We need to realize that missions are always bigger than organizations, just as organizations are always bigger than the individuals who run them. Missions need effort and the mind provides the purpose. Seen this way, consider, which department or ministry will take man to Mars and build a habitat there? Can 200,000 MW of electric power be generated by isolated efforts in thermal, hydroelectric, nuclear and non-conventional sectors without an integrated effort? Can the second green revolution happen without agricultural scientists, bio-technologists and irrigation experts working together? Without proper diagnostic facilities in clinics and affordable drugs reaching our masses, our biotechnology laboratories and medical councils will continue to perpetuate each other's survival without serving the purpose of their existence: to set in place the most advanced medical facilities and make these available to the people at reasonable prices.

I have dwelt upon my own experiences that made me aware of the energy field which is created by a vision. It is a power that arises from deep within you. This power is the basis for the movement towards excellence we saw at the time of independence. I have been touched by this power on many occasions while facing a challenge. Pre-independence India reverberated with it. It helped us humble a mighty empire.

Jamshedji Nusserwanji Tata brought the steel industry to India even though the British rulers were not favourably disposed to the idea. Acharya P.C. Ray nurtured the chemical and pharmaceutical industries. We saw the birth of many great institutions like the Indian Institute of Science, Bangalore, started by J.N. Tata, the Banaras Hindu University established by Pandit Madan Mohan Malaviya, and Aligarh Muslim University set up by Sir Syed Ahmad Khan. Some of the progressive maharajas too set up universities, as in

Baroda. There are many examples. In all these cases, the motivation was to see India come up in the world, to demonstrate that 'India can do it'.

Are we in a position to continue that work, revive that spirit of enterprise? Shall we ever see cars designed and manufactured in India dotting the roads in Frankfurt or Seoul? Or Indian satellite launch vehicles place communication, weather and remote sensing satellites of other nations in orbit? Or see India build power stations for the USA, Japan and China? The possibility will remain remote if we stay with the present trend of low aim.

Today we are witnessing good progress in the software sector but almost all of the hardware is imported. Can we rise higher on the value scale there? Can India design an operating system that will become a household name in the world of computers? Our exports consist to a large extent of low-value raw material such as iron ore and alumina. Can we not convert these into a wide range of products that find an international market? We have hundreds of defence production industries but why does India not manufacture and market the Main Battle Tank, missiles, aircraft, guns and other defence equipment? We have the most important core competence in the form of our multifaceted manpower and basic infrastructure. What is that we don't have?

Let us think what prevents us in undertaking such challenges. We have to analyse how we can give a new dimension to our style of functioning, by cutting across the individual interests of various ministries and even industries and institutions, to follow an integrated action plan. The motive force has to be love for the country. We need a vision that is shared by the entire nation.

In the drive for development, some states are faring better than others in the country. Bright young entrepreneurs have energized the national technology scene. Bangalore, Chennai, Mumbai, Delhi and Hyderabad are hubs of business activity. But even though the IT sector is a very visible area of success and has brought in some capital investment, in terms of overall development this is not enough. Even if you take up the IT area as a mission, manpower is the most important need. Those living away from the cities must also have access to a good education to join the talent pool. And this should happen fast.

My visits to the northeastern states—Tripura and Assam—and to Jharkhand showed me our untapped potential. Tripura's economy rests on forest products, including bamboo cultivation. It is rich in mineral wealth, as also in natural gas. But the transport facilities are in bad shape. It is difficult to travel, interact and organize business. There is isolation. In Jharkhand too there is mineral wealth besides its resources in terms of forestry products and handicrafts, all of which need to be developed. In Assam, there is no shortage of resources and the state has good educational infrastructure. All the ingredients required for a developed economy are there but there is insurgency and unrest among people. A focussed mission will integrate people.

States such as Tamil Nadu, Andhra Pradesh, Punjab and Karnataka have made me realize that much can be achieved once efforts are made to channel development funds for improvement in areas such as education and health. These and other states can become good examples of economic development.

Our intellectual forums, political platforms, academic institutions and chambers of commerce are full of discussion and debate. There is noise, a lot of it in fact. There are endless debates, arguments, hypotheses, and theories, and yet there is little progress. However, the theme of a developed India is not discussed in board rooms and technology conferences. I want all of us—institutions, political parties, industries, communities, families, individuals—at every level to take full responsibility for what is good or bad in our situation, for what we possess and that which we do not. This would mean that we stop blaming others for the circumstances we find ourselves in. Taking responsibility also means a willingness to exercise our abilities to the fullest. This will make us worthy of enjoying the benefits that come with effort.

What I have tried to tell you in this book is that we must be aware of our higher self and view ourselves as citizens of a developed nation. We are a great civilization and each one of us born here must trust in the wisdom of this civilization. Our scriptures tell us that there is no barrier between us and the world, that we are the world just as the world is in us. It is for you to put yourself in tune with the music of the universe.

There are a few points I would like to mention.

The needs of a nation's people are bigger and much more important than any other considerations. The mission of Parliament is that it has to be alive and dynamic over issues vital to the existence of our very nationhood. Our freedom did not come as a gift. The whole country struggled for decades to achieve the first vision of independence, so we have to protect it. There were excellent leaders in all walks of life—science, education and industry. To preserve this freedom from intruders and others who would compromise it is our bounden duty and not a matter of choice and convenience. No ideology is above the security and prosperity of our country. No agenda is more important than harmony among the people.

Students should get ready to transform India into a developed nation. Ignite your minds and think big.

A teacher once said, 'Give me a five-year-old child. After seven years, no God or Devil will be able to change the child.' Will all teachers be such gurus?

The administrators have a great opportunity to link the people and political leaders. They should always take decisions that are good for the people. I believe it is only executives like empowered district collectors who can assist transformation. The state-Central integrated fund has to be deployed in mission mode programmes.

Fifty years after independence, the results of scientific effort have not reached the people to the extent required. It is time the advances in science and technology are deployed in a big way to transform rural life.

Global competition is on, be it WTO, competition from multinationals or China. For industrialists, competing with high-performance and cost-effective products will result in growth for the industry. Competitiveness and innovation are the two pillars of industrial growth. Industries by working together can generate multinational institutions, reversing the present trend.

The IT community, by its innovativeness has given India stature in the world. India is a competitive nation in IT today. IT must be used for healthcare, telemedicine, to remove illiteracy, generate skills and for e-governance and tele-education. Transform the nation into a knowledge society with IT as the linking tool.

Finally, the farmers have given this country surplus food with their sweat. Time has come for two events to take place in agriculture sector. One, the value addition of all agriculture products. The second is to improve the quality of agriculture products and compete in the world market. Above all marketing itself is a great business tool; we have to create a new cadre for this purpose. These steps will bring relief to the farmers.

And to God the Almighty! Make my people sweat. Let their toil create many more Agnis that can annihilate evil. Let my country prosper in peace. Let my people live in harmony. Let me go to dust as a proud citizen of India, to rise again and rejoice in its glory.

EPILOGUE

I was thinking what can summarize the book aptly. I recall reading a story on the Internet about a conversation between two babies—Ego and Spirit—while in the womb.

Spirit says to Ego, 'I know you are going to find this hard to accept, but I believe there is life after birth.'

Ego responds, 'Don't be foolish. Look around you. This is all there is. Why must you always be thinking about something beyond this reality? Accept your lot in life.'

Spirit quietens down for a while, but not for long. 'Ego, now don't get angry, but I also believe that there is a Mother.'

'A Mother!' Ego laughs. 'How can you say that? You've never seen a Mother, you don't know what Mother is. Why can't you accept that this is all there is? You are here alone with me. This is your reality.'

'Ego,' Spirit begs, 'please listen. What about those constant pressures we both feel, those movements that make us so uncomfortable sometimes, the feeling that we are being squeezed in as we grow? I think we shall soon have a new life, that we shall see light.'

Ego replies, 'You have never seen light. How do you know what it is? These pressures and darkness is what life is about.'

Spirit tries not to bother Ego again but cannot resist one last try. 'Ego,' she says, 'I will not bother you again. But I do believe that after all this discomfort not only shall we see light but also experience the bliss of meeting Mother.'

Ego's reply is, of course, that Spirit is truly mad.

What I want to tell the people of my country through this book is that they must never be content with that which has been presented to them in the last fifty years since our independence. When I was on the verge of completing this book, somebody raised a very important point with me. While addressing 1,500 students at Presidency College, Chennai, on the theme 'Nation Has to Have Vision', a series of questions came from the students on national development, political leadership, science and technology's contribution, education and the learning process and so on. After the session, coming out of the auditorium, a visibly happy gathering of students was trying to reach me to shake hands. While I was manoeuvring to leave, suddenly one young student pushed through the crowd and thrust a crumpled paper in my hand. I put it in my pocket and read it in the car. My mind got elevated with the power of the message from T. Saravanan doing M.Phil Zoology at Presidency College. I would like to share it with all of you.

The letter read:

'Dear Sir

'The full power of a banyan tree is equal to the power in the seeds of the tree. In a way both of us, you and me, are the same. But we exhibit our talents in different forms. A few of the seeds directly flourish as banyan trees and many seeds die. Sometimes, the seeds, due to certain circumstances and environmental conditions, get damaged and become part of the soil as manure, making the next generation stronger and more powerful, thus exhibiting its aim of achieving greater heights.

'You have worked for the country and helped many scientists, engineers and knowledge workers. Can you tell me how you ensured that their abilities were not wasted or their growth was not stunted prematurely as some of the seed? In this service, what is the percentage of success you can claim?'

My reply the same day said:

'Dear Saravanan,

'I have read and re-read your powerful message and question many times. I spent twenty years in ISRO and twenty years in DRDO making rockets, launch vehicles and missiles. I have seen many successes and also a few failures. I have worked with many scientists, engineers and technicians as united teams to achieve goals in a short time. The combined power of the team has seen those successes and learnt from the failures. I could see some of my team members excelling me in knowledge and deed. This gave me immense happiness.'

Saravanan's message gives all of us a tremendous responsibility. Leaders must ensure that the younger generation is better than them and not subject them to circumstances that will stunt their growth. Above all, protection of the young from failures in scientific developments and constant encouragement are essential to ensure that scientists, technologists or those working in any field grow and work for the nation.

I would like to conclude this book with an answer to one last question, asked of me on Id. The question was: What prayer did you say on this occasion?

I replied, apart from praying for the health and happiness of my teachers, friends and relatives, I said this prayer:

'O Almighty, create thoughts and actions in the minds of the people of my nation so that they live united.

Help all religious leaders of my country give strength to the people to combat the forces of division.

Embed the thought "Nation is bigger than the Individual" in the minds of the leaders and people.

O God bless my people to work and transform the country into a prosperous nation soon.'

I have conveyed the message overleaf to nearly 40,000 school children in Chennai, Porbandar, Rajkot, Jamshedpur, Bhubaneshwar, Dindigul, Abu Road, Anand, Udaipur and many other places so far. I hope to reach 100,000 young minds before August 2003. When thousands recite this, I see the developed India.

Song of Youth

Me and My Nation-India

As a young citizen of India,
armed with technology, knowledge and love for my nation,
I realize, small aim is a crime.

I will work and sweat for a great vision,
the vision of transforming India into a developed nation
powered by economic strength with value system.

I am one of the citizens of a billion,
only the vision will ignite the billion souls.
It has entered into me,
the ignited soul compared to any resource,
is the most powerful resource
on the earth, above the earth and under the earth.

I will keep the lamp of knowledge burning
to achieve the vision—Developed India.

REFERENCES

1. *Wings of Fire: An Autobiography,* A.P.J. Abdul Kalam with Arun Tiwari. Universities Press (India) Pvt. Ltd., 1999.

2. *India 2020: A Vision for the New Millennium,* A.P.J. Abdul Kalam and Y.S. Rajan. Viking, 1998.

3. *Man the Unknown,* Alexis Carrel.

4. *Thirukkural,* Thiruvalluvar.

5. *Light from Many Lamps,* Lillian Eichler Watson. Fireside, 1988.

6. *Chandra: A Biography of S. Chandrasekhar,* Kameshwar C. Wali. University of Chicago Press, 1992.

7. *The Horse That Flew,* Chidanand Rajghatta. HarperCollins India, 2001.

8. *Empires of the Mind,* Denis Waitley. Nicholas Brealey Publishing, 1995.

9. *An Unfinished Dream,* Dr Verghese Kurien. Tata McGraw Hill, 1997.

10. *Manifest Your Destiny,* Dr Wayne W. Dyer. HarperCollins, 1997.

11. *Consilience,* Edward O. Wilson. Vintage Books, 1999.

12. *India as Knowledge Superpower,* Task Force Report to Planning Commission, 2001.

13. *Technology Vision 2020,* TIFAC Task Force Reports, 1996.

14. 'A New Knowledge Society', Dr A.P.J. Abdul Kalam, 2000.

15. Report on 'Rurbanization', Prof. P.V. Indiresan, 2000.

INDEX